PROVE IT

From
Conversation *to* Presentation

She has a passion for fashion. And she can prove it.

GUNTHER BREAUX

Improve your voice, not your memory.

No teacher talk on the first day of class!

OMG! What about the syllabus? Attendance? Grading? What about the usual blah blah blah and leave early?

Those days are over. Read the syllabus online or watch the video. Classes are for conversations.

INSTRUCTIONS

1. **Sit in pairs. Turn your book sideways.**
   You use this page, your partner will use the other page. Each page has 12 different questions.
2. **Ask a question, any question.**
   Talk a while. Then ask follow up questions.
   Then ask, What about you?
3. **It's a conversation, not a police interrogation.**
   If a conversation starts, go with it.

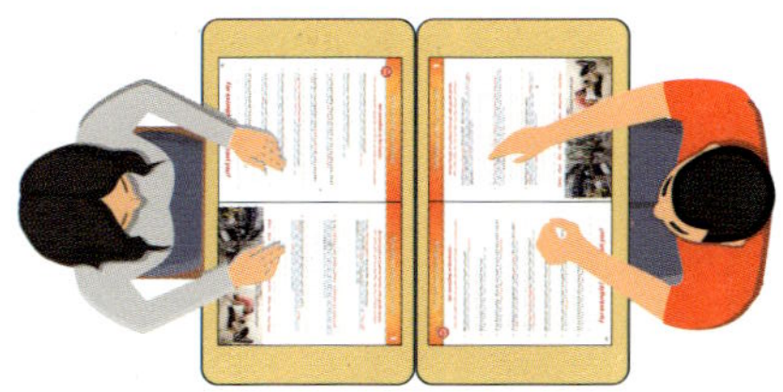

What's your major?
Do you like your major?
What's your dream major?

Are talented at anything?
Music, art, sports, computer games?
Did you ever win a contest?

Will you take a gap year?
Will you take extra courses and try to finish early?

Where do you live?
Where's your hometown?
How often do you go home?

How many courses are you taking have this semester?
How many hours?

Do you like team projects?
Do you contribute the most, or least? Are you a deadbeat?

Did you ever get a scholarship?
What is your hardest course this semester? Easiest course?

How do you get to school?
How long does it take? Would you like to live in a dormitory?

What is your hardest class?
What was your hardest class last semester? Favorite class?

Are you a morning person or evening person?
When is your best time to study?

How many times did you take the Soonung?
Are you good at taking tests?

What high school did you go to?
How often do you see your high school friends?

Me too! Where? When? Why? Who? How? How often? • For example? WHAT ABOUT YOU?

First day Meet & Mingle

You've heard teachers talk for 10 years. It's your turn to talk.

You're going to meet a new classmate every 5 minutes, and talk about your major, classes and club.

This is Speed Dating

You get a new partner every 5 minutes.

Everybody's speaking half the time, half the time your partner's a better speaker.

Speak on the first day of class?

Is this legal? Yes.

But, is talking to strangers about my major, classes and club academic? YES.

What's your MBTI?
Do you believe in personality types?
Are you a loner or a joiner?

How many universities did you apply to?
What school was your first choice?

Which do you like more, your club or your major?
High school or university?

What's your dream job?
What's your realistic Plan B job?
Have you done your military service?

Have you ever traveled abroad?
Where exactly? When did you go?
How long did you stay?

Are you an Apple person or Windows person?
What kind of phone do you have?

What did you do last winter/summer vacation?
Do you like to travel?

What does your father do?
What does your mother do?
Are they workaholics?

Did you ever have a part-time job?
Did you save or spend?

For important assignments, do you use a desktop or laptop?
Do you have a long attention span?

Do you belong to a club?
How often do you meet? Where?
How many members?

What did you do last weekend?
What will you do after class?
What will you do this weekend?

Me too! Where? When? Why? Who? How? How often? • For example? WHAT ABOUT YOU?

CONTENTS

Part 1

From Conversation to Presentation

Cover in Class

Do the book at home, speak in class.

To make a presentation,
you need some basic information before you start.

However, if information is introduced unit by unit,
you will not get some important information until the last unit.
Therefore, this book has two parts:

Part 2

How to Make a Presentation, from A to Z

Cover at Home

The Website has Audio, Video Instructions,
and MS Word, PowerPoint and Keynote templates.
proveit123.com

Make and watch presentations at home, talk about them in class.

From CONVERSATION

Personality-Type Conversations

1

Each unit begins with 10 Personality-type questions

Are you an introvert or an extrovert?

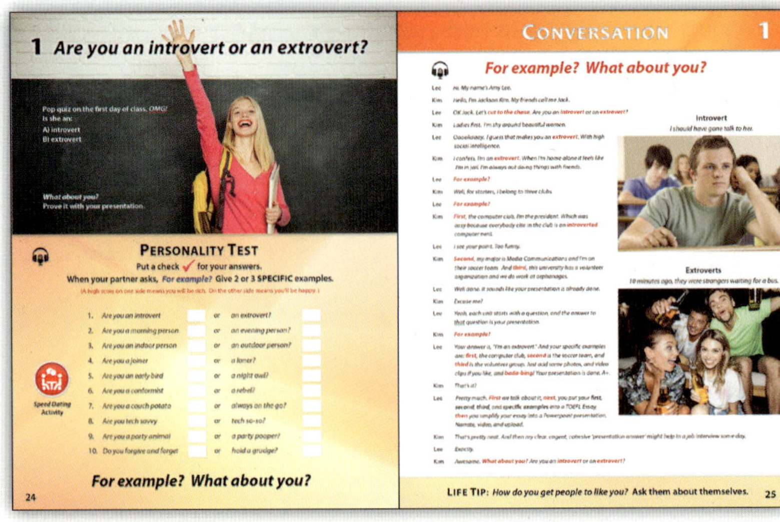

Write it, then say it

2

The questions are answered and used in

Pair Conversations

Idioms and Quiz

3

Up your game using

Idioms and Vocabulary

in longer and better answers

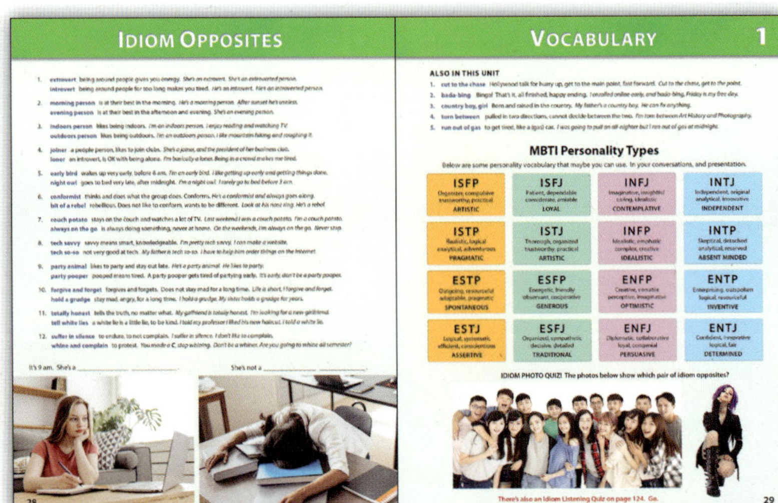

To Presentation

4

The question is answered with an

Elevator Speech

which can be part of your

TOEFL Essay

Elevator Speech | Format

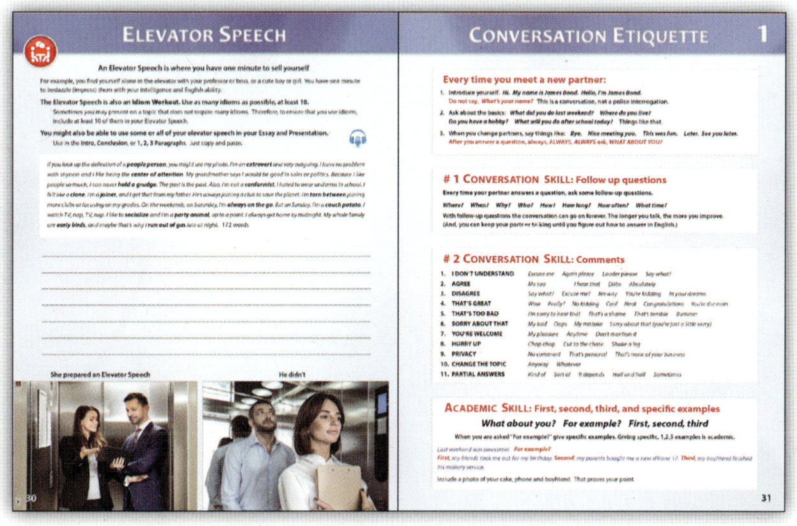

5

TOEFL Essay

is the format and transcript of your

PPT Presentation

Copy and paste from MS Word to PPT

TOEFL Essay | Outline

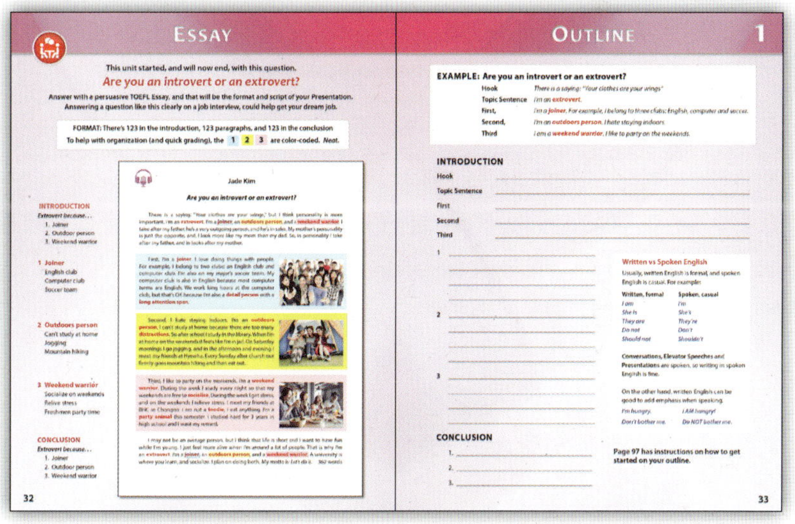

6

Each unit ends with your 3-minute

Video Presentation Answer

I'm an extrovert because first, second, third

It's your life, you know the specific details

Format | Feedback Conversation

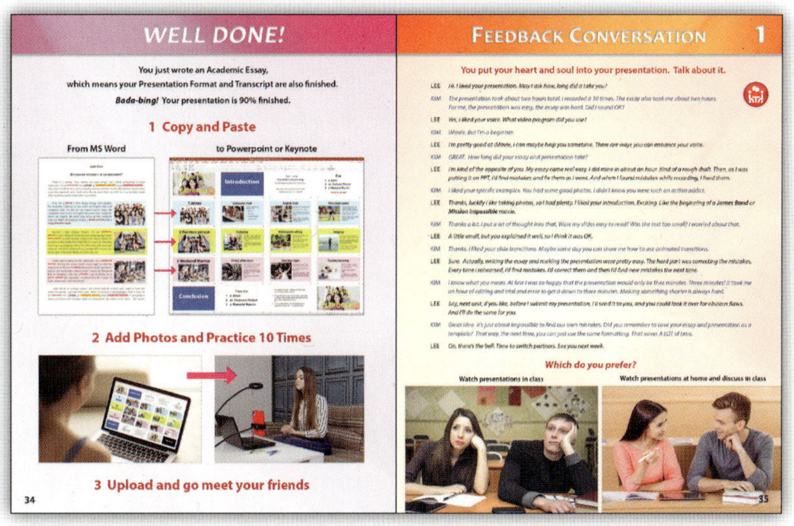

TYPES OF PRESENTATIONS

VOICE

Narrated Video

No memorizing. Focus on your voice. Clear, articulate speaking.

TALKING HEAD

Zoom Presentation

Put your face in the video.

WHOLE BODY

Video presentation

Use an empty classroom. Your (or your partners) can video.

IN PERSON

TED Talk

Memorize, note cards, eye contact, the works.

Even if you're presenting in person, you should still make a narrated video first.

You will find and correct your mistakes, improve your voice, and have a permanent record.

And, watching videos at home frees up class time for conversations about presentations.

Topic Choices

In each unit you have a choice of topics.

We suggest you use a topic that you already know. Yourself.

1. Each unit is about a different facet of yourself. You are the world's expert.
2. Answer a question that might be asked on a job interview. For example: *Are you an introvert or an extrovert?*
3. There is no research. The time saved can be spent on improving your voice, vocabulary, and presentation.

1	**PERSONALITY**	***Are you an introvert or an extrovert?*** What's your MBTI? • Are you a conformist or a rebel? • Are you a joiner or a loner? Are you a morning person or an evening person? Are you an indoors or an outdoors person?
2	**EDUCATION**	***Are you an idea person or a detail person?*** Why did you choose your major? • What courses are you taking this semester? Do you have a long or short attention span? • Are you a bookworm or a slacker?
3	**TECHNOLOGY**	***Are you tech savvy or tech so-so? Are you Apple or Windows?*** What is your most important tech device, app, program, SNS? The three most important? What is the most important app and program in your major? The three most important?
4	**ROMANCE**	***Do you believe in love at first sight, or true love takes time?*** Is your boy or girlfriend high or low maintenance? • Do you take more than you give? What are the most important qualities in a partner: Face, body, personality, money? Why?
5	**WORKING**	***Are you a workaholic or a slacker?*** What's your life philosophy: YOLO, FIRE, DINK? • Is your first impulse to save or to spend? Are you a team player or a lone wolf? • Would you rather be house rich or cash rich?
6	**FREE TIME**	***What's more important, your major or your club?*** Are you a couch potato or an action addict? • Are you a party animal or a party pooper? What gives you stress: grades, professors, parents, friends? How do you relieve stress?

The goal of each presentation is to enhance your abilities to answer a job interview question.
One of your presentation videos could be part of a job interview submission package.

This book is about you. It's your life, you know the specific details.
No research, no memorizing. Much practice.

Pick an interesting topic and use your voice to make it more interesting.

What's the difference between a model and a movie star?

A movie star can speak.

Their voice put them into a higher, richer, more famous orbit.

This is Scarlett Johansson, famous Hollywood actress.

A few years ago, there was a movie called ***Her***. It's about a man who falls in love with his computer's voice.

They used Scarlett's voice. She's never seen in the movie. They could have used anyone's voice. The voice artist did not need to be good looking. However, they chose Scarlett's voice.

Why? She has a great voice.

She was chosen because of her voice, not her looks. In fact, movies that she has appeared in have made more money than the movies of any other movie star.

She's number 1 in the world in highest career film sales.

> **POP QUIZ!** ***Already? OMG!***
>
> ***What do all actors and actresses have in common?***
>
> A) They are good looking
>
> B) They have a nice personality
>
> C) They have a good voice

Looks, Personality, Voice

Those are your top 3 tools you have to sell yourself in life

We suggest you use this course to improve your voice. As your voice improves, so does your English.

> **Many movie stars do voices for animated movies and documentaries.** ***Why?*** They have a great voice.
> Below are more movies stars who do the voices for animation movies. You may think, ***Hey, those are good looking people.***
> Yes, they are. However, they were chosen for their voice, not their looks. Their great voice helps make them successful.

Emma Stone

Julia Roberts

Anne Hathaway

Jon Hamm

Dwayne Johnson

Steven Yeun

THE GOAL

Improve your voice, not your memory

This isn't about researching a topic and presenting it to class.

The goal is not to make you comfortable speaking in front a large number of people.
The goal is not making good eye contact and using good body language.
The goal is not a speech where you glance at note cards 90% of the time.
The goal is not a memorized speech. That takes way too much time.
You have already covered all that in other classes.

The goal is SPEAKING ability

Clear, confident, articulate, TV-announcer speaking ability

Gee, how do I get that?

1 Do what professionals do. Read. Newscasters sound professional because they are reading.
2 Practice 10 times.

Your brain can only do so much at one time. When you read you can:

FOCUS ON YOUR VOICE

Pronounce correctly, add emphasis, stress, drama, joy. Persuade with your voice.

And Practice 10 Times

Every time you practice you will find mistakes, and make mistakes. Fix them.
After 10 times, your presentation, and your voice, will be greatly improved.

No research, no memorizing. Much practice.

Each Unit Has 3 Phases

College Conversations

Speed Dating Pair Conversations

Longer Conversations

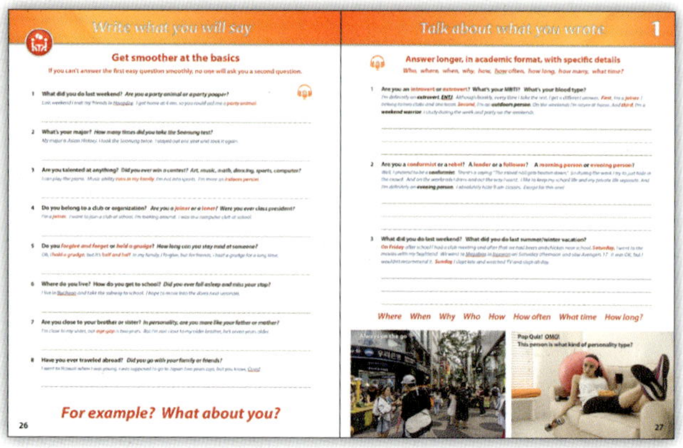

Up your game with Idioms & Elevator Speech

Idioms & Vocabulary & Quiz

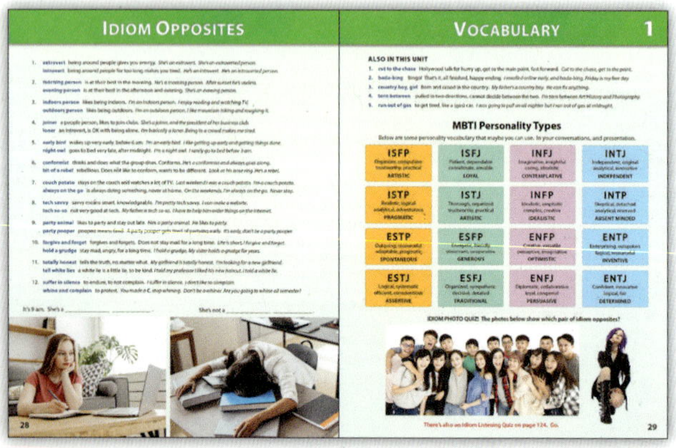

Elevator Speech

Format

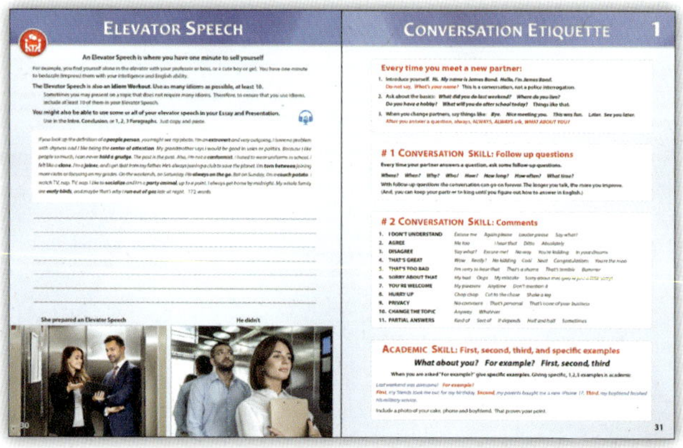

Academic Presentation

TOEFL Essay

Outline

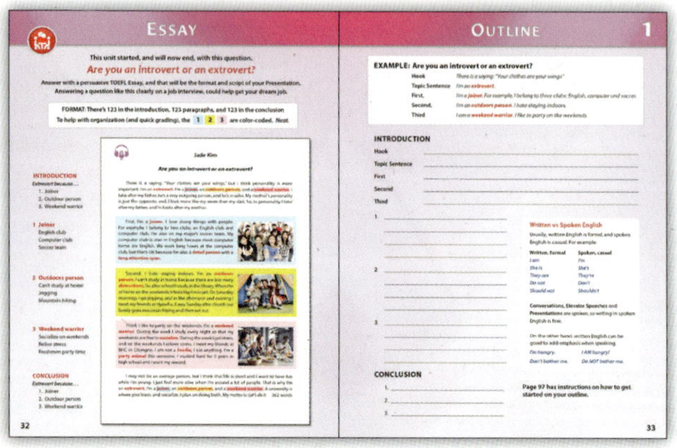

Presentation

Feedback Conversation

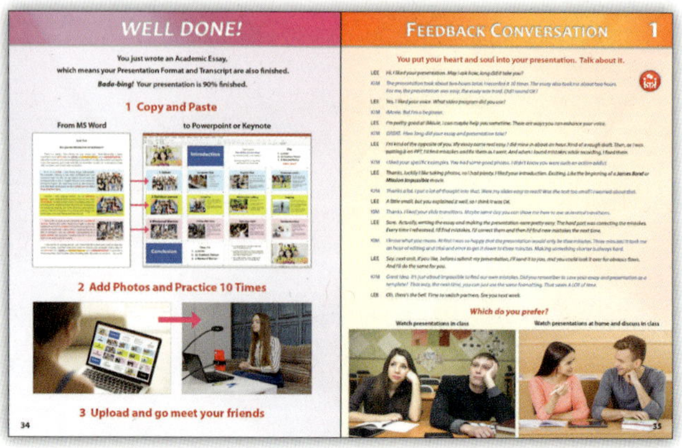

TYPICAL UNIT

1 Do the book at home

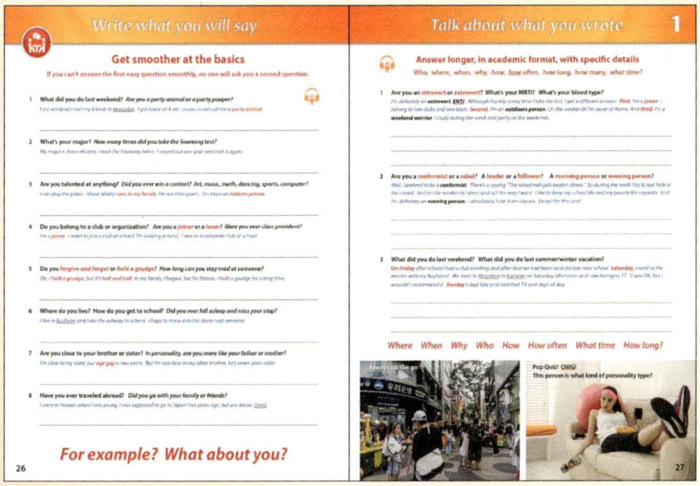

2 Speak in class

3 Make your presentation at home

4 Rehearse 10 times and upload on Friday

5 Watch over the weekend

6 Discuss in class on Monday

This is a new century with new technology. Record and watch at home, discuss in class.

Speed Dating Conversations

A new topic every 2 weeks, a new partner every seven minutes

Many partners make you smoother, better partners make you better. ***Simple.***

1. Meet, greet, introduce yourself, and chat. After 7 minutes, the teacher yells, ***SWITCH!***
2. Students seated on the inside say, ***Bye, Gotta go, Nice meeting you, See you later***, and move on.
3. Next class you'll do it again, better, smoother, with new partners.

Half your partners are better speakers, and better at making presentations. Learn from them.
When conversations are about presentations, both improve.

ELEVATOR SPEECH

Impress me. You have 1 minute.

An **Elevator Speech** is where you sell yourself in one or two minutes. For example, you're in the elevator with your professor or boss, and they ask you a question, just to be polite. You seize the opportunity to give a smart, articulate answer, and impress them with your knowledge, personality, and English ability.

For example: If you're a guy trying to meet a girl, you might start off saying something like:
Hi, I'm Jack. I have a PhD from Harvard, I've won the Nobel Prize, I'm an Olympic champion, and a tech billionaire. And I teach orphans on the weekends. (Jack is a world-class liar, but he does sound interesting.)

This is also an Idiom Workout. Try to use as many as possible.

*If you look up the definition of a **people person**, you might see my photo. I'm an **extrovert** and very **outgoing**. I have no problem with shyness and I like being the **center of attention**. My grandmother says I would be good in sales or politics. Because I like people so much, I can never **hold a grudge**. The past is the past. Also, I'm not a **conformist**. I hated to wear uniforms in school. I felt like a **clone**. I'm a **joiner**, and I get that from my father. He's always joining a club to save the planet. I'm **torn between** joining more clubs or focusing on my grades. On the weekends, on Saturday, I'm **always on the go**. But on Sunday, I'm a **couch potato**. I watch TV, nap, TV, nap. I like to **socialize** and I'm a **party animal**, up to a point. I always get home by midnight. My whole family are **early birds**, and maybe that's why I **run out of gas** late at night.* 172 words

She prepared an Elevator Speech, and hung out near the elevator.

Practicing your elevator speech is excellent practice for your presentation.

And,
your Speech can be used in class
to start Speed Dating conversations.

You wrote it. Talk about it.

From ESSAY

Your TOEFL Essay is your Presentation Format and Transcript

An academic essay is a persuasive essay. It gives evidence, it tries to prove something. It tries to convince you by giving specific examples, using photos, charts, data.

For example:

1. **Nuclear power is good (or bad), because of 1, 2, 3.** Followed by 3 examples, with photos and data.
2. **I'm an introvert (or extrovert), because of 1, 2, 3.** Followed by 3 examples, with photos and video.

For successful people, life is a thesis essay:

1. ***Mother, you should give me a bigger allowance, because of 1, 2, 3.***
2. ***Jenni, you should go out on a date with me because of 1, 2, 3.***
3. ***Harvard, you should accept me because of 1, 2, 3.***
4. ***Google, you should hire me because of 1, 2, 3.***

ESSAY, with specific examples from your own life

Jade Kim

Are you an introvert or an extrovert?

Introduction
I'm an extrovert because of 1,2,3

There is a saying: "Your clothes are your wings," but I think personality is more important. I'm an **extrovert**. I'm a **joiner**, an **outdoors person**, and a **weekend warrior**. I take after my father, he's a very outgoing person, and he's in sales. My mother's personality is just the opposite, and, I look more like my mom than my dad. So, in personality I take after my father, and in looks after my mother.

1 Joiner

First, I'm a **joiner**. I love doing things with people. For example, I belong to two clubs: an English club and computer club. I'm also on my major's soccer team. My computer club is also in English because most computer terms are English. We work long hours at the computer club, but that's OK because I'm also a **detail person** with a **long attention span**.

2 Outdoors person

Second, I hate staying indoors. I'm an **outdoors person**. I can't study at home because there are too many **distractions**. So after school I study in the library. When I'm at home on the weekends it feels like I'm in jail. On Saturday mornings I go jogging, and in the afternoon and evening I meet my friends at Hyewha. Every Sunday after church our family goes mountain hiking and then eat out.

3 Weekend warrior

Third, I like to party on the weekends. I'm a **weekend warrior**. During the week I study every night so that my weekends are free to **socialize**. During the week I get stress, and on the weekends I relieve stress. I meet my friends at BHC in Chongno. I am not a **foodie**, I eat anything. I'm a **party animal** this semester. I studied hard for 3 years in high school and I want my reward.

Conclusion
Thus, I'm an extrovert because of 1,2,3

I may not be an average person, but I think that life is short and I want to have fun while I'm young. I just feel more alive when I'm around a lot of people. That is why I'm an **extrovert**. I'm a **joiner**, an **outdoors person**, and a **weekend warrior**. A university is where you learn, and socialize. I plan on doing both. My motto is: *Let's do it.* 362 words

Copy

To Presentation

Your Presentation is a multimedia version of your Essay

TOEFL Essays and Presentations have the exact same persuasive, academic format.

1. **Introduction**, which introduces the three reasons. *First, second, third.*
2. **First, second, third paragraphs**, with specific details
3. **Conclusion**, which summarizes the three reasons. *First, second, third.*

That's it. Academic format with personal examples. It's your life, you know the specific details.

Your **TOEFL Essay** and **Presentation** are the **SAME THING**, different medium.

Copy and paste

PRESENTATION, with the same specific examples. Copy and paste. *Wow! That was easy.*

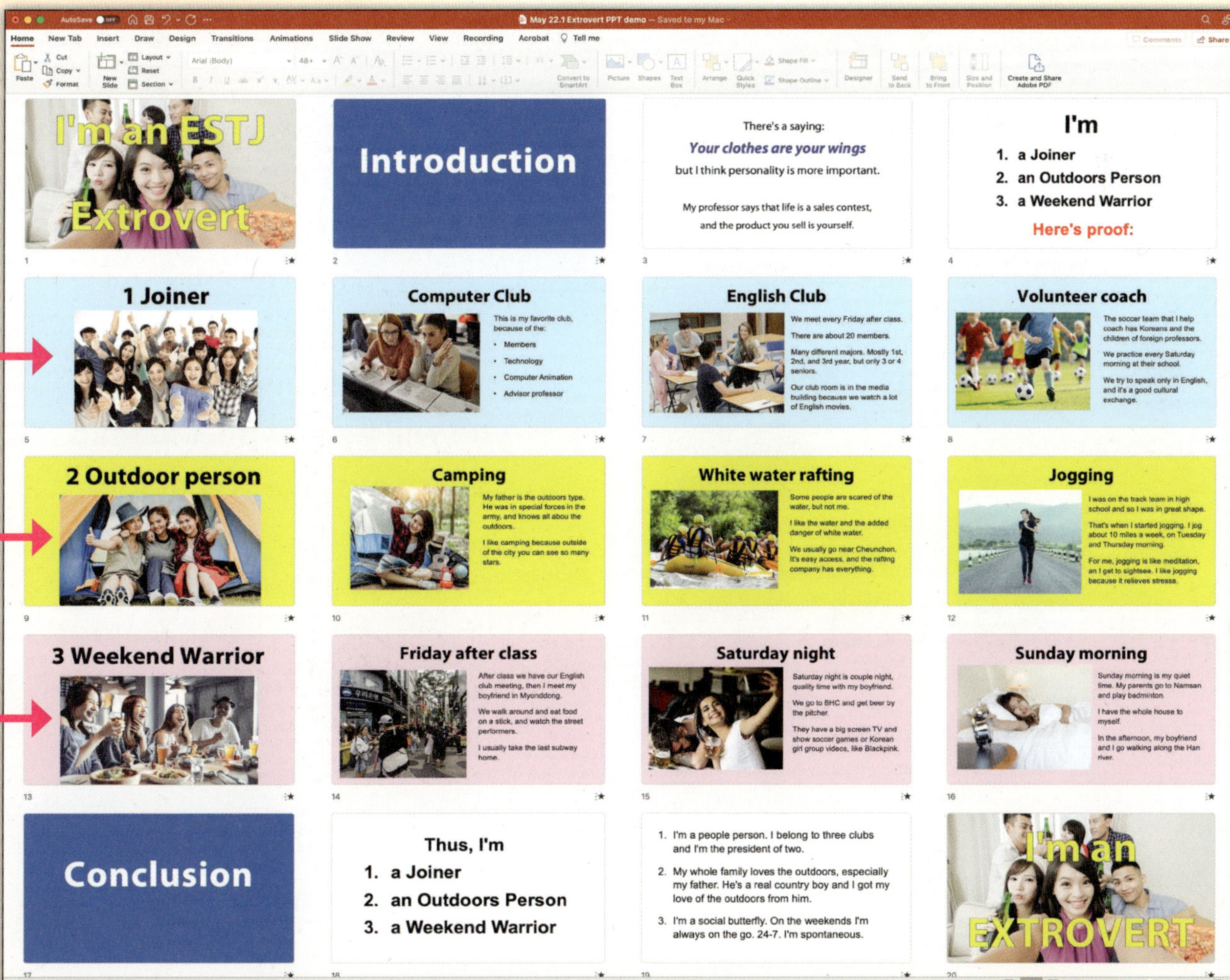

and Paste

Conversation Overview

1 At home, *Write what you will say.*

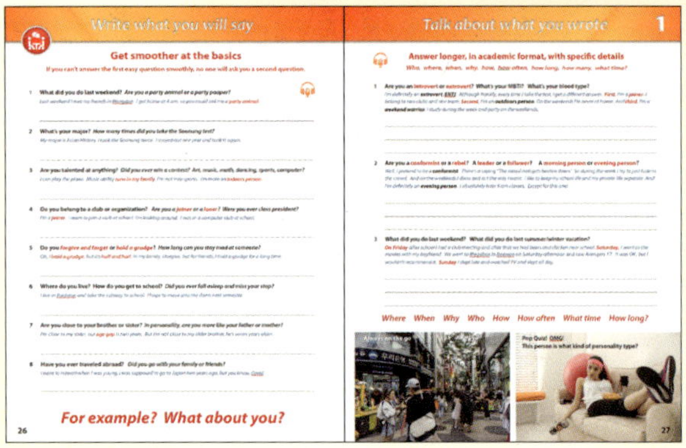

30 minutes of homework

2 In class, *Talk about what you wrote.*

generates 3 hours of conversations.

Just add partners.

3 The Test, *Transcribe what you said*

While transcribing,
you will hear, type and read
every mistake you made.

Typical Results

	Average words per turn	Total words I spoke
Midterm test	8.6	436
Final test	15.5	523
Improvement	**80%**	**20%**

Your speaking improves
and you can prove it.

PARTNERS, NOT GRAMMAR

Many partners make you smoother, better partners make you better.

Test partners of similar ability gives fair and accurate testing.

This is the Class

The class is pair conversations. Speed Dating.
You get a new topic every 2 weeks, and a new partner every 7 minutes.
Everybody's speaking half the time, and half the time your partner's a better speaker.

This is the Test

Three students of similar ability have a 17-minute conversation.
Record it with your phone, transcribe what you said, and self-correct.
The first test measures your ability, the second test measures your improvement.

Why is there a conversation test? **That's what makes you have conversations.**

Presentation Overview

Here's a new way of teaching Presentation

1 Add conversation to your presentation class
2 Use narrated videos instead of in person presentations
3 Use personally relevant topics. It's your life, you know the specific details

Why?

1 Conversation and Presentation are a great fit

- Improving one improves both
- Students should have conversation ability in the topic they're presenting

2 Narrated video presentations

- Find your mistakes
- Improve your voice
- Have a permanent record
- Free up class time for conversations
- Are an important school and work skill

3 Use personally relevant topics

No research Spend that time making a better, high-tech presentation.
No memorizing Spend that time improving your speaking and pronunciation.

4 Presentation Options

- For units 1, 2, 3, make a video. For your midterm test, select your favorite, and present that in class.
- Likewise, for units 4, 5, 6, make a video, and then present your favorite in class for your final exam.
- Units 1, 2, 3 can be video, and units 4, 5, 6 can be in person. (Improve your voice, then the whole package)

Each unit has 12 pages, 6 components

and takes 2 weeks to cover. That's 1 hour of homework per week.

1	**Pair Conversations**	Write what you will say, talk about what you wrote.
2	**Idioms and Vocabulary**	Includes **MBTI** Personality Types.
3	**Elevator Speech**	Makes speaking longer and smoother, and includes at least 10 idioms
4	**TOEFL Essay**	Is the format and transcript of the Presentation. Copy and paste.
5	**Presentation**	Is a multimedia version of the Essay. Add photos, charts, audio and video.
6	**Feedback Conversation**	You put your heart and soul into your presentation, talk about it.

There's no *blah blah blah* teacher talk on how to make a presentation

Information is in the book and website. Read and watch as many times as you like.
Do the book at home. Make and watch presentations at home. Speak in class.

Improve your voice, not your memory

Old School

Teacher talk

Research

Memorize

Present

21st Century

Discuss in class

Make

Narrate

Discuss in class

If presentations are in class, narrated videos are excellent preparation

Personality Test

Put a check ✓ for your answers.
When your partner asks *For example?* Give a **SPECIFIC** example.

1 BASIC PERSONALITY

Are you an introvert		*or an extrovert?*	
Are you a couch potato		*or always on the go?*	
Are you a morning person		*or an evening person?*	

2 EDUCATION

Do you have a long		*or short attention span?*	
Are you an idea person		*or a detail person?*	
Are you an underachiever		*or an overachiever?*	

3 TECH

Are you tech savvy		*or tech so-so?*	
Are you Apple		*or Windows?*	
Would you rather play sports		*or a video game?*	

4 ROMANTIC

Do you believe in love at first sight		*or true love takes time?*	
Is your boy / girl friend: high		*or low maintenance?*	
What's more important, face		*or body?*	

5 WORKING

Are you a workaholic		*or a slacker?*	
Are you a lone wolf		*or team player?*	
Are you a self-starter		*or do you watch the clock?*	

6 FREE TIME

Are you a party animal		*or a party pooper?*	
Are you a weekend warrior		*or a social drinker?*	
Are you the life of the party		*or a wet blanket?*	

For example? What about you?

CONVERSATION

This is a conversation, not a police investigation. When a conversation starts, *go with it*.

Lee *Hi. My name's Amy Lee.*

Kim *Hello, I'm Jackson Kim. My friends call me Jack.*

Lee *OK Jack. First, some basics. Where's your hometown?*

Kim *Kwangju. We lived there until I was 10, then we moved to Seoul. What about you?*

Lee *I'm from Seoul. First we lived in Nowon, and then we moved to Mapo. Which is where I live now. Where do you live?*

Kim *We live in Mokdong on the purple line. What's your major? And what year are you?*

Lee *Business Administration. I'm a Sophomore. And you?*

Kim *Me too! Well, actually Public Administration. But close. I'm a junior.*

Lee *Cool. So, are you an* ***introvert*** *or* ***extrovert****? Wait, what's your* ***MBTI****?*

Kim *I'm* ***ISFP: kind, spontaneous, accommodating****.* ***What about you?***

Lee *I took the test twice and came up with two different types.* ***INFP: idealistic, empathetic*** *and* ***complex****. And* ***ENTJ: confident, innovative*** *and* ***logical****.* ***INFP*** *says I'm complex, maybe that's what they mean.*

Kim *Could be. How about this, are you an* ***idea person*** *or a* ***detail person****?*

Lee *Wait, that question is in the second batch.*

Kim *Hey. I'm* ***ISFP****.* ***Spontaneous****. Go with it.*

Lee *OK fine. I'm a* ***detail person****. I haven't met many* ***idea people*** *in Business. A lot of accountant types. What about you?*

Kim *I know what you mean about accountant types. As for me, I'm* ***half and half****. My hobby is computer animation, which requires ideas, but to get anything done requires a detail person.*

Lee *Why didn't you major in Computer Graphics or something like that?*

Kim *My grades weren't good enough, but I'll try to make that my second major.*

E xtroverts
are energized by people, enjoy a variety of tasks, and are good at multitasking.

S ensors
are realistic, focus on the facts and details, and use common sense.

T hinkers
make decisions using logic, and value honesty, consistency and fairness

J udgers
are organized and like to stick to plans and are good with following rules.

I ntroverts
like working alone, and prefer a deliberate pace and focus on one task.

N intuitives
prefer to focus on the big picture, easily see patterns, and seek creative solutions.

F eelers
sensitive and cooperative, decide based on personal values, and how others feel.

P erceivers
like to keep their options open, act spontaneously and are flexible.

1 Are you an introvert or an extrovert?

Pop quiz on the first day of class. *OMG!*
Is she an:

A) introvert
B) extrovert

What about you?
Prove it with your presentation.

Personality Test

Put a check ✓ for your answers.

When your partner asks, ***For example?*** Give 2 or 3 **SPECIFIC** examples.

(A high score on one side means you will be rich. On the other side means you'll be happy.)

1.	*Are you an introvert*	☐	*or*	*an extrovert?*	☐
2.	*Are you a morning person*	☐	*or*	*an evening person?*	☐
3.	*Are you an indoor person*	☐	*or*	*an outdoor person?*	☐
4.	*Are you a joiner*	☐	*or*	*a loner?*	☐
5.	*Are you an early bird*	☐	*or*	*a night owl?*	☐
6.	*Are you a conformist*	☐	*or*	*a rebel?*	☐
7.	*Are you a couch potato*	☐	*or*	*always on the go?*	☐
8.	*Are you tech savvy*	☐	*or*	*tech so-so?*	☐
9.	*Are you a party animal*	☐	*or*	*a party pooper?*	☐
10.	*Do you forgive and forget*	☐	*or*	*hold a grudge?*	☐

Speed Dating Activity

For example? What about you?

For example? What about you?

Lee *Hi. My name's Amy Lee.*

Kim *Hello, I'm Jackson Kim. My friends call me Jack.*

Lee *OK Jack. Let's* ***cut to the chase****. Are you an* ***introvert*** *or an* ***extrovert****?*

Kim *Ladies first. I'm shy around beautiful women.*

Lee *Ooookaaay. I guess that makes you an* ***extrovert****. With high social intelligence.*

Kim *I confess, I'm an* ***extrovert****. When I'm home alone it feels like I'm in jail. I'm always out doing things with friends.*

Lee ***For example?***

Kim *Well, for starters, I belong to three clubs.*

Lee ***For example?***

Kim ***First****, the computer club, I'm the president. Which was easy because everybody else in the club is an* ***introverted*** *computer nerd.*

Lee *I see your point. Too funny.*

Kim ***Second****, my major is Media Communications and I'm on their soccer team. And* ***third****, this university has a volunteer organization and we do work at orphanages.*

Lee *Well done. It sounds like your presentation is already done.*

Kim ***Excuse me?***

Lee *Yeah, each unit starts with a question, and the answer to that question is your presentation.*

Kim ***For example?***

Lee *Your answer is, "I'm an extrovert." And your specific examples are:* ***first****, the computer club,* ***second*** *is the soccer team, and* ***third*** *is the volunteer group. Just add some photos, and video clips if you like, and* ***bada-bing****! Your presentation is done. A+.*

Kim *That's it?*

Lee *Pretty much.* ***First*** *we talk about it,* ***next****, you put your* ***first****,* ***second****,* ***third****, and* ***specific examples*** *into a TOEFL Essay,* ***then*** *you simplify your essay into a Powerpoint presentation. Narrate, video, and upload.*

Introvert

I should have gone talk to her.

Extroverts

10 minutes ago, they were strangers waiting for a bus.

Kim *That's pretty neat. And then my clear, cogent, cohesive 'presentation answer' might help in a job interview some day.*

Lee *Exactly.*

Kim *Awesome.* ***What about you?*** *Are you an* ***introvert*** *or an* ***extrovert?***

LIFE TIP: *How do you get people to like you?* **Ask them about themselves.**

Write what you will say

Get smoother at the basics

If you can't answer the first easy question smoothly, no one will ask you a second question.

1 **What did you do last weekend?** ***Are you a party animal or a party pooper?***
Last weekend I met my friends in Hongdae. I got home at 4 am, so you could call me a ***party animal****.*

2 **What's your major?** ***How many times did you take the Soonung test?***
My major is Asian History. I took the Soonung twice. I stayed out one year and took it again.

3 **Are you talented at anything?** ***Did you ever win a contest? Art, music, math, dancing, sports, computer?***
I can play the piano. Music ability ***runs in my family****. I'm not into sports. I'm more an* ***indoors person****.*

4 **Do you belong to a club or organization?** ***Are you a joiner or a loner? Were you ever class president?***
I'm a ***joiner****. I want to join a club at school, I'm looking around. I was in a computer club at school.*

5 **Do you** ***forgive and forget*** **or** ***hold a grudge*****?** ***How long can you stay mad at someone?***
Oh, I ***hold a grudge****, but it's* ***half and half****. In my family, I forgive, but for friends, I hold a grudge for a long time.*

6 **Where do you live? How do you get to school?** ***Did you ever fall asleep and miss your stop?***
I live in Bucheon and take the subway to school. I hope to move into the dorm next semester.

7 **Are you close to your brother or sister?** ***In personality, are you more like your father or mother?***
I'm close to my sister, our ***age gap*** *is two years. But I'm not close to my older brother, he's seven years older.*

8 **Have you ever traveled abroad?** ***Did you go with your family or friends?***
I went to Hawaii when I was young. I was supposed to go to Japan two years ago, but you know, Covid.

For example? What about you?

Talk about what you wrote

Answer longer, in academic format, with specific details

Who, where, when, why, how, how often, how long, how many, what time?

1 **Are you an introvert or extrovert? What's your MBTI? What's your blood type?**

*I'm definitely an **extrovert**, **ENTJ**. Although frankly, every time I take the test, I get a different answer. **First**, I'm a **joiner**. I belong to two clubs and one team. **Second**, I'm an **outdoors person**. On the weekends I'm never at home. And **third**, I'm a **weekend warrior**. I study during the week and party on the weekends.*

____

____

____

2 **Are you a conformist or a rebel? A leader or a follower? A morning person or evening person?**

*Well, I pretend to be a **conformist**. There's a saying "The raised nail gets beaten down." So during the week I try to just hide in the crowd. And on the weekends I dress and act the way I want. I like to keep my school life and my private life separate. And I'm definitely an **evening person**. I absolutely hate 9 am classes. Except for this one!*

____

____

____

3 **What did you do last weekend? What did you do last summer/winter vacation?**

***On Friday** after school I had a club meeting and after that we had beers and chicken near school. **Saturday,** I went to the movies with my boyfriend. We went to Megabox in Itaewon on Saturday afternoon and saw Avengers 17. It was OK, but I wouldn't recommend it. **Sunday** I slept late and watched TV and slept all day.*

____

____

____

Where When Why Who How How often What time How long?

Idiom Opposites

1. **extrovert** being around people gives you energy. *She's an extrovert. She's an extroverted person.*
   introvert being around people for too long makes you tired. *He's an introvert. He's an introverted person.*
2. **morning person** is at their best in the morning. *He's a morning person. After sunset he's useless.*
   evening person is at their best in the afternoon and evening. *She's an evening person.*
3. **indoors person** likes being indoors. *I'm an indoors person. I enjoy reading and watching TV.*
   outdoors person likes being outdoors. *I'm an outdoors person. I like mountain hiking and roughing it.*
4. **joiner** a people person, likes to join clubs. *She's a joiner, and the president of her business club.*
   loner an introvert, is OK with being alone. *I'm basically a loner. Being in a crowd makes me tired.*
5. **early bird** wakes up very early, before 6 am. *I'm an early bird. I like getting up early and getting things done.*
   night owl goes to bed very late, after midnight. *I'm a night owl. I rarely go to bed before 3 am.*
6. **conformist** thinks and does what the group does. Conforms. *He's a conformist and always goes along.*
   bit of a rebel rebellious. Does not like to conform, wants to be different. *Look at his nose ring. He's a rebel.*
7. **couch potato** stays on the couch and watches a lot of TV. *Last weekend I was a couch potato. I'm a couch potato.*
   always on the go is always doing something, never at home. *On the weekends, I'm always on the go. Never stop.*
8. **tech savvy** savvy means smart, knowledgeable. *I'm pretty tech savvy. I can make a website.*
   tech so-so not very good at tech. *My father is tech so-so. I have to help him order things on the Internet.*
9. **party animal** likes to party and stay out late. *He's a party animal. He likes to party.*
   party pooper pooped means tired. A party pooper gets tired of partying early. *It's early, don't be a party pooper.*
10. **forgive and forget** forgives and forgets. Does not stay mad for a long time. *Life is short, I forgive and forget.*
    hold a grudge stay mad, angry, for a long time. *I hold a grudge. My sister holds a grudge for years.*
11. **totally honest** tells the truth, no matter what. *My girlfriend is totally honest. I'm looking for a new girlfriend.*
    tell white lies a white lie is a little lie, to be kind. *I told my professor I liked his new haircut. I told a white lie.*
12. **suffer in silence** to endure, to not complain. *I suffer in silence. I don't like to complain.*
    whine and complain to protest. *You made a* ***C****, stop whining. Don't be a whiner. Are you going to whine all semester?*

It's 9 am. She's a ______________ ______________ .

She's not a ______________ ______________ .

ALSO IN THIS UNIT

1. **bada-bing** Bingo! That's it, all finished, happy ending. *I enrolled online early, and bada-bing, Friday is my free day.*
2. **country boy, girl** Born and raised in the country. *My father's a country boy. He can fix anything.*
3. **cut to the chase** Hollywood talk for hurry up, get to the main point, fast forward. *Cut to the chase, get to the point.*
4. **run out of gas** to get tired, like a (gas) car. *I was going to pull an all-nighter but I ran out of gas at midnight.*
5. **torn between** pulled in two directions, cannot decide between the two. *I'm torn between Art History and Photography*

MBTI Personality Types

Below are some personality vocabulary that maybe you can use. In your conversations, and presentation.

ISFP Organizer, compulsive trustworthy, practical **ARTISTIC**	**ISFJ** Patient, dependable considerate, amiable **LOYAL**	**INFJ** Imaginative, insightful caring, idealistic **CONTEMPLATIVE**	**INTJ** Independent, original analytical, innovative **INDEPENDENT**
ISTP Realistic, logical analytical, adventurous **PRAGMATIC**	**ISTJ** Thorough, organized trustworthy, practical **ARTISTIC**	**INFP** Idealistic, emphatic complex, creative **IDEALISTIC**	**INTP** Skeptical, detached analytical, reserved **ABSENT MINDED**
ESTP Outgoing, resourceful adaptable, pragmatic **SPONTANEOUS**	**ESFP** Energetic, friendly observant, cooperative **GENEROUS**	**ENFP** Creative, versatile perceptive, imaginative **OPTIMISTIC**	**ENTP** Enterprising, outspoken logical, resourceful **INVENTIVE**
ESTJ Logical, systematic efficient, conscientious **ASSERTIVE**	**ESFJ** Organized, sympathetic decisive, detailed **TRADITIONAL**	**ENFJ** Diplomatic, collaborative loyal, congenial **PERSUASIVE**	**ENTJ** Confident, innovative logical, fair **DETERMINED**

IDIOM OPPOSITE PHOTO QUIZ! The photos below show which pair of idiom opposites?

There's also an Idiom Listening Quiz on page 124. Go.

ELEVATOR SPEECH

An Elevator Speech is where you have one minute to sell yourself

For example, you find yourself alone in the elevator with your professor or boss, or a cute boy or girl. You have one minute to bedazzle (impress) them with your intelligence and English ability.

The Elevator Speech is also an Idiom Workout. Use as many idioms as possible, at least 10.

Sometimes you may present on a topic that does not require many idioms. Therefore, to ensure that you use idioms, include at least 10 of them in your Elevator Speech.

You might also be able to use some or all of your elevator speech in your Essay and Presentation.

Use in the **Intro**, **Conclusion**, or **1, 2, 3 Paragraphs**. Just copy and paste.

If you look up the definition of a ***people person****, you might see my photo. I'm an* ***extrovert*** *and very* ***outgoing****. I have no problem with shyness and I like being the* ***center of attention****. My grandmother says I would be good in sales or politics. Because I like people so much, I can never* ***hold a grudge****. The past is the past. Also, I'm not a* ***conformist****. I hated to wear uniforms in school. I felt like a* ***clone****. I'm a* ***joiner****, and I get that from my father. He's always joining a club to save the planet. I'm* ***torn between*** *joining more clubs or focusing on my grades. On the weekends, on Saturday, I'm* ***always on the go****. But on Sunday, I'm a* ***couch potato****. I watch TV, nap, TV, nap. I like to* ***socialize*** *and I'm a* ***party animal****, up to a point. I always get home by midnight. My whole family are* ***early birds****, and maybe that's why I* ***run out of gas*** *late at night.* 172 words

____

____

____

____

____

____

____

She prepared an Elevator Speech

He didn't

Every time you meet a new partner:

1. **Introduce yourself.** ***Hi. My name is James Bond. Hello, I'm James Bond.***
   Do not say, ***What's your name?*** This is a conversation, not a police interrogation.
2. **Ask about the basics:** ***What did you do last weekend? Where do you live? Do you have a hobby? What will you do after school today?*** Things like that.
3. **When you change partners, say things like:** ***Bye. Nice meeting you. This was fun. Later. See you later.***
   After you answer a question, always, ALWAYS, ***ALWAYS*** ask, ***WHAT ABOUT YOU?***

1 CONVERSATION SKILL: Follow up questions

Every time your partner answers a question, ask some follow-up questions.

Where? When? Why? Who? How? How long? How often? What time?

With follow-up questions the conversation can go on forever. The longer you talk, the more you improve. (And, you can keep your partner talking until you figure out how to answer in English.)

2 CONVERSATION SKILL: Comments

1.	**I DON'T UNDERSTAND**	*Excuse me Again please Louder please Say what?*
2.	**AGREE**	*Me too I hear that Ditto Absolutely*
3.	**DISAGREE**	*Say what? Excuse me? No way You're kidding In your dreams*
4.	**THAT'S GREAT**	*Wow Really? No kidding Cool Neat Congratulations You're the man*
5.	**THAT'S TOO BAD**	*I'm sorry to hear that That's a shame That's terrible Bummer*
6.	**SORRY ABOUT THAT**	*My bad Oops My mistake Sorry about that (you're just a little sorry)*
7.	**YOU'RE WELCOME**	*My pleasure Anytime Don't mention it*
8.	**HURRY UP**	*Chop chop Cut to the chase Shake a leg*
9.	**PRIVACY**	*No comment That's personal That's none of your business*
10.	**CHANGE THE TOPIC**	*Anyway Whatever*
11.	**PARTIAL ANSWERS**	*Kind of Sort of It depends Half and half Sometimes*

ACADEMIC SKILL: First, second, third, and specific examples

What about you?   For example?   First, second, third

When you are asked "For example?" give specific examples. Giving specific, 1,2,3 examples is academic.

Last weekend was awesome! ***For example?***
First*, my friends took me out for my birthday.* ***Second****, my parents bought me a new iPhone 17.* ***Third****, my boyfriend finished his military service.*

Include a photo of your cake, phone and boyfriend. That proves your point.

ESSAY

This unit started, and will now end, with this question.

Are you an introvert or an extrovert?

Answer with a persuasive TOEFL Essay, and that will be the format and script of your Presentation.
Answering a question like this clearly on a job interview, could help get your dream job.

(There are more topic choices on page 9)

FORMAT: There's 123 in the introduction, 123 paragraphs, and 123 in the conclusion
To help with organization (and quick grading), the **1** **2** **3** are color-coded. *Neat.*

INTRODUCTION
Extrovert because...
1. Joiner
2. Outdoor person
3. Weekend warrior

1 Joiner
English club
Computer club
Soccer team

2 Outdoors person
Can't study at home
Jogging
Mountain hiking

3 Weekend warrior
Socialize on weekends
Relive stress
Freshmen party time

CONCLUSION
Extrovert because...
1. Joiner
2. Outdoor person
3. Weekend warrior

Jade Kim

Are you an introvert or an extrovert?

There is a saying: "Your clothes are your wings," but I think personality is more important. I'm an **extrovert**. I'm a **joiner**, an **outdoors person**, and a **weekend warrior**. I take after my father, he's a very outgoing person, and he's in sales. My mother's personality is just the opposite, and, I look more like my mom than my dad. So, in personality I take after my father, and in looks after my mother.

First, I'm a **joiner**. I love doing things with people. For example, I belong to two clubs: an English club and computer club. I'm also on my major's soccer team. My computer club is also in English because most computer terms are English. We work long hours at the computer club, but that's OK because I'm also a **detail person** with a **long attention span**.

Second, I hate staying indoors. I'm an **outdoors person**. I can't study at home because there are too many **distractions**. So after school I study in the library. When I'm at home on the weekends it feels like I'm in jail. On Saturday mornings I go jogging, and in the afternoon and evening I meet my friends at Hyewha. Every Sunday after church our family goes mountain hiking and then eat out.

Third, I like to party on the weekends. I'm a **weekend warrior**. During the week I study every night so that my weekends are free to **socialize**. During the week I get stress, and on the weekends I relieve stress. I meet my friends at BHC in Chongno. I am not a **foodie**, I eat anything. I'm a **party animal** this semester. I studied hard for 3 years in high school and I want my reward.

I may not be an average person, but I think that life is short and I want to have fun while I'm young. I just feel more alive when I'm around a lot of people. That is why I'm an **extrovert**. I'm a **joiner**, an **outdoors person**, and a **weekend warrior**. A university is where you learn, and socialize. I plan on doing both. My motto is: *Let's do it.* 362 words

EXAMPLE: Are you an introvert or an extrovert?

Hook	*There is a saying: "Your clothes are your wings"*
Topic Sentence	*I'm an* ***extrovert****.*
First,	*I'm a* ***joiner****. For example, I belong to three clubs: English, computer and soccer.*
Second,	*I'm an* ***outdoors person****. I hate staying indoors.*
Third	*I am a* ***weekend warrior****. I like to party on the weekends.*

INTRODUCTION

Hook ____________________

Topic Sentence ____________________

First ____________________

Second ____________________

Third ____________________

1 ____________________

____

____

____

2 ____________________

____

____

____

3 ____________________

____

____

____

Written vs Spoken English

Usually, written English is formal, and spoken English is casual. For example:

Written, formal	Spoken, casual
I am	*I'm*
She is	*She's*
They are	*They're*
Do not	*Don't*
Should not	*Shouldn't*

Conversations, Elevator Speeches and **Presentations** are spoken, so writing in spoken English is fine.

On the other hand, written English can be good to add emphasis when speaking.

I'm hungry.	*I AM hungry!*
Don't bother me.	*Do NOT bother me.*

CONCLUSION

1. ____________________
2. ____________________
3. ____________________

Page 97 has instructions on how to get started on your outline.

WELL DONE!

You just wrote an Academic Essay,
which means your Presentation Format and Transcript are also finished.
Bada-bing! Your presentation is 90% finished.

1 Copy and Paste

From MS Word

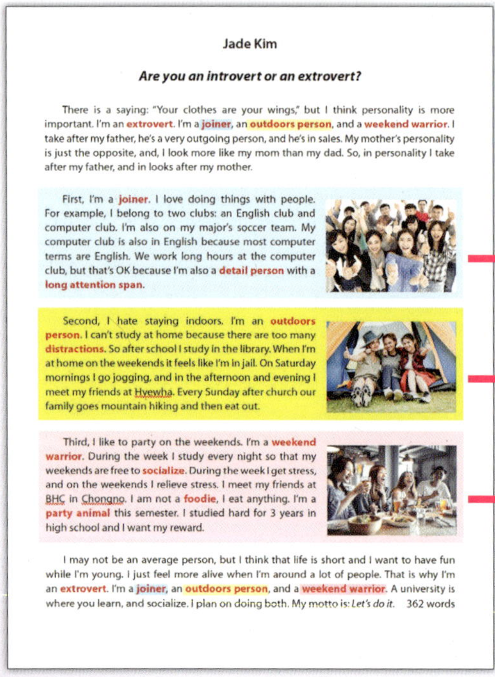

Jade Kim

Are you an introvert or an extrovert?

There is a saying: "Your clothes are your wings," but I think personality is more important. I'm an **extrovert**. I'm a **joiner**, an **outdoors person**, and a **weekend warrior**. I take after my father, he's a very outgoing person, and he's in sales. My mother's personality is just the opposite, and, I look more like my mom than my dad. So, in personality I take after my father, and in looks after my mother.

First, I'm a **joiner**. I love doing things with people. For example, I belong to two clubs: an English club and computer club. I'm also on my major's soccer team. My computer club is also in English because most computer terms are English. We work long hours at the computer club, but that's OK because I'm also a **detail person** with a **long attention span**.

Second, I hate staying indoors. I'm an **outdoors person**. I can't study at home because there are too many **distractions**. So after school I study in the library. When I'm at home on the weekends it feels like I'm in jail. On Saturday mornings I go jogging, and in the afternoon and evening I meet my friends at Hyewha. Every Sunday after church our family goes mountain hiking and then eat out.

Third, I like to party on the weekends. I'm a **weekend warrior**. During the week I study every night so that my weekends are free to **socialize**. During the week I get stress, and on the weekends I relieve stress. I meet my friends at BHC in Chongno. I am not a **foodie**, I eat anything. I'm a **party animal** this semester. I studied hard for 3 years in high school and I want my reward.

I may not be an average person, but I think that life is short and I want to have fun while I'm young. I just feel more alive when I'm around a lot of people. That is why I'm an **extrovert**. I'm a **joiner**, an **outdoors person**, and a **weekend warrior**. A university is where you learn, and socialize. I plan on doing both. My motto is: *Let's do it.* 362 words

to Powerpoint or Keynote

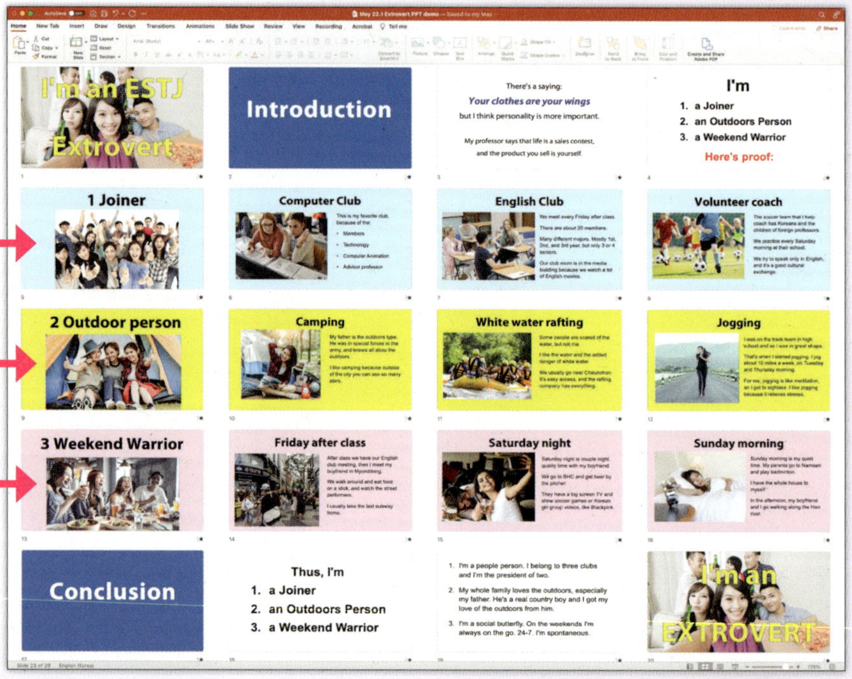

2 Add Photos and Practice 10 Times

3 Upload and go meet your friends

You put your heart and soul into your presentation. Talk about it.

LEE *Hi. I liked your presentation. May I ask how, long did it take you?*

KIM *The presentation took about two hours total. I recorded it 10 times. The essay also took me about two hours. For me, the presentation was easy, the essay was hard. Did I sound OK?*

LEE *Yes, I liked your voice. What video program did you use?*

KIM *iMovie. But I'm a beginner.*

LEE *I'm pretty good at iMovie, I can maybe help you sometime. There are ways you can enhance your voice.*

KIM *GREAT. How long did your essay and presentation take?*

LEE *I'm kind of the opposite of you. My essay came real easy. I did mine in about an hour. Kind of a rough draft. Then, as I was putting it on PPT, I'd find mistakes and fix them as I went. And when I found mistakes while recording, I fixed them.*

KIM *I liked your specific examples. You had some good photos. I didn't know you were such an* **action addict**.

LEE *Thanks, luckily I like taking photos, so I had plenty. I liked your introduction. Exciting. Like the beginning of a* ***James Bond*** *or* ***Mission Impossible*** *movie.*

KIM *Thanks a lot. I put a lot of thought into that. Were my slides easy to read? Was the text too small? I worried about that.*

LEE *A little small, but you explained it well, so I think it was OK.*

KIM *Thanks. I liked your slide transitions. Maybe some day you can show me how to use animated transitions.*

LEE *Sure. Actually, writing the essay and making the presentation were pretty easy. The hard part was correcting the mistakes. Every time I rehearsed, I'd find mistakes. I'd correct them and then I'd find new mistakes the next time.*

KIM *I know what you mean. At first I was so happy that the presentation would only be thee minutes. Three minutes! It took me an hour of editing and trial and error to get it down to three minutes. Making something shorter is always hard.*

LEE *Say, next unit, if you like, before I submit my presentation, I'll send it to you, and you could look it over for obvious flaws. And I'll do the same for you.*

KIM *Great idea. It's just about impossible to find our own mistakes. Did you remember to save your essay and presentation as a template? That way, the next time, you can just use the same formatting. That saves A LOT of time.*

LEE *Oh, there's the bell. Time to switch partners. See you next week.*

Which do you prefer?

Watch presentations in class

Watch presentations at home and discuss in class

2 Are you an idea person or a detail person?

What about you?
Prove it with your presentation.

Oh really. Well, here's a Personality Test

Put a check ✓ for your answers.

When your partner asks, ***For example?*** Give two or three **SPECIFIC** examples.

1.	*Are you an idea person*	☐	*or*	*a detail person?*	☐
2.	*Do you have a long*	☐	*or*	*short attention span?*	☐
3.	*Are you a brainiac*	☐	*or*	*slow on the uptake?*	☐
4.	*Is your major professor an easy grader*	☐	*or*	*a hard grader?*	☐
5.	*Are you an underachiever*	☐	*or*	*overachiever?*	☐
6.	*Do you cram for exams*	☐	*or*	*prepare ahead of time?*	☐
7.	*Are you a bookworm*	☐	*or*	*a slacker?*	☐
8.	*Are you more of a jock*	☐	*or*	*a nerd?*	☐
9.	*Are your parents strict*	☐	*or*	*lenient about your grades?*	☐
10.	*Do you procrastinate*	☐	*or*	*decide quickly?*	☐

For example? What about you?

CONVERSATION 2

Sort of • Sometimes • It depends • Half and half

Not every answer is Yes or No, black or white. Some things are shades of gray.

Lee *Hi. Are you new in class? I didn't see you last week.*

Kim *Yes, I'm new. I was in another presentation class, but the professor talked the whole time, so I switched.*

He's a little slow on the uptake

Lee *Super. My name's Adele Lee.*

Kim *I'm James Kim. Nice to meet you. What's your major?*

Lee *My major's accounting, and you?*

Kim *My major is computer animation. So, are you an* ***idea person*** *or a* ***detail person****?*

Lee *Du-uh. Accountants are* ***detail people****.*

Kim *Oh yeah, right.*

Lee *What about you? Are you an* ***idea person*** *or a* ***detail person****?*

Kim ***Half and half.***

Lee ***For example?***

Kim *Well,* ***first****, computer animation requires ideas, creativity. But* ***second****, it also requires details. With computer coding, if one little period is off, nothing works.*

Lee *Ah, I see. Well, are you creative or very creative?*

Kim ***That depends****.*

Lee ***For example?***

Kim *If I'm working on a computer game, I'm* ***kind of*** *creative. But if I'm working on a homework project for class and I get to choose my own topic, I'm very creative.*

Lee *When you work on animation, is your goal an A+, or to satisfy yourself? Do you want to fulfill your vision, regardless of how much the teacher likes it.*

Kim ***That depends.*** *My major professor, he is good! I try to please him, because I know if he likes it, it will be great. But, I have had other professors, who gave a lot of homework, but not a lot of feedback.*

Lee *Got it. I know the type.*

Kim *So, Accounting. Do you have a* ***long*** *or* ***short attention span****?*

Lee *I'm sorry. What was your question? Kidding.*

Kim *Funny.*

Lee *It's kind of* ***half and half****. I can work on something for 12 hours, if I can take a break every two hours.* ***What about you?***

Write what you will say

Get smoother at the basics

If you can't answer an easy first question smoothly, no one will ask you a second question.

1 **Did you study, sleep, or party last weekend? Are you a party animal or a party pooper?**
Last weekend I hit the books. I have a test in my major tomorrow. I'll pull an all-nighter tonight.

2 **What's your major? What's your minor, or second major?**
My major is Pharmacy. I'm good at chemistry, that's why I chose it. My minor is Biology.

3 **Do you have a long or short attention span? Do you procrastinate or decide quickly?**
I have a long attention span, if I have a lot of coffee. I can study for two hours at one sitting.

4 **Do you prefer a team project or to work alone? On a team project do you do the most, or least?**
I prefer to work alone. I do not take classes that have team projects, unless I have to in a major course.

5 **Do you study during the week or wait till the weekends? Where do you study?**
I like to keep up with my studies during the week so that the weekends are mine. I study at the school library.

6 **Are you more of a bookworm or a slacker? Did you ever drop a class? Are you a quitter?**
In high school I was a bookworm, but now I'm a slacker. I never dropped a class, but once I should have.

7 **Did you ever tutor a student? Did you ever have a tutor? Do you go to an academy now?**
I tutored a student once, but her grades did not go up and her mom fired me. Not my fault.

8 **Do you belong to a club? It is more of a study club or a social club?**
I belong to a club in my major, we do volunteer work. But, we are kind of light on volunteering, and heavy on socializing.

For example? What about you?

Answer longer, in academic format, with specific details

Who, where, when, why, how, how often, how long, how many, what time?

1 **Are you an idea person or a detail person?**

*Well, I thought I was a great combination of an **idea** and **detail person** before I got to college. But there's a lot of really creative idea people here. So, I admit that I'm a **detail person**. **First**, I have a **long attention span**. **Second**, I'm good at detail things like computer coding. And **third**, I'm a real good proofreader for my friends. I catch a lot of their mistakes.*

____

____

____

2 **Why did you chose your major? Did your parents give you any advice?**

***First**, I've always been interested in computer graphics. My specific interest is programming software for computer games. **Second**, I'm pretty sure that with computer skills I'll be able to get a good job. And **finally**, I think the trend is that I may be able to work remotely, from home, or anywhere. I think Computer Science is a good fit for me.*

____

____

____

3 **What courses are you taking this semester? Do you have a free day? Do you belong to a club?**

*I have three **major** courses: **Math**, **Accounting** and **Economics**. Three **required** courses: **Korean History**, **English** and **Computer**. And one **elective** course: **History of Art**. I don't have a free day, but all my classes are in the afternoon, and I really like that. I belong to the Tae kwon do club. We meet every Wednesday evening, for workouts and socializing.*

____

____

____

Kind of   Sort of   Sometimes   It depends   Half and half

Where   When   Why   Who   How   How often   What time   How long?

Idiom Opposites

1. **idea person** creative, has many ideas, a movie director. *I'm an idea person. I have some ideas for computer games.*
   detail person writes computer code, or an accountant. *He's a detail person. He can write code for hours.*
2. **long attention span** can focus and study for a long time with no break. *She has a long attention span.*
   short attention span cannot focus for a long time. *I have a short attention span. I need a break every half hour.*
3. **brainiac** very smart. *She's a brainiac. She sees something once and she knows it.*
   slow on the uptake, slow learner takes a long time, to master something. *He's a cute guy, but slow on the uptake.*
4. **brown nose** to praise or compliment someone way too much. *He's a brown-nose. He's a brown-noser.*
   badmouth to say bad things about someone. *Stop badmouthing him. Do not badmouth your professor.*
5. **easy grader** very lenient on grading. *I took his class because I heard he's an easy grader. Half the class got an A.*
   hard grader hard, strict on grading. *She's a hard grader, the highest grade in class was a B minus.*
6. **underachiever** smart, but performs below their ability. *My mom told me I was an underachiever.*
   overachiever average smart, but studies very hard. *He was an overachiever in high school, but now he's worn out.*
7. **cram** to try to study very much in a short period of time. *I usually cram. I crammed three hours right before the test.*
   prepare ahead of time prepare in advance. *I hate to cram the night before, so I always prepare ahead of time.*
8. **bookworm** studies very much, their nose is always in a book. *He's a bookworm. He's always in the library.*
   slacker lazy student or worker, underachiever. *He's a slacker. I slacked off last semester. Stop slacking off.*
9. **jock** good at sports, but not smart. *He's a jock. He got an athletic scholarship, and he needs help in some classes.*
   nerd smart, but bad at sports. *He's a computer nerd. He's a nice guy, but doesn't have many social skills.*
10. **strict, bad cop** strict. *My parents are strict about my grades. Especially my dad, he plays the bad cop.*
    lenient, good cop lenient. *My mother's the good cop. After my father fusses at me, she secretly gives me money.*
11. **procrastinate** to delay, take a long time, to make a decision. *I procrastinate. I procrastinated. He procrastinates.*
    decide quickly decide quickly. *She's doesn't procrastinate, she decides quickly, and goes to work.*
12. **bail out**, **quit** to quit, to jump out of a plane with a parachute. *Her tests were too hard so I bailed. I bailed out.*
    stick it out to endure, not quit. *I like the professor so I'll stick it out. I stuck it out and made an A.*

MBTI College Majors

Type	Majors	Type	Majors
ISFP	Anthropology, Animal Science	INFJ	Psychology, Philosophy and Logic
ISTP	Computer Science, Biochemistry	INFP	Psychology, English
ESTP	Criminal Justice, Chemical Engineering	ENFP	Languages, Journalism, Music
ESTJ	Economics, Finance, Business	ENFJ	Public Policy, Education, Acting
ISFJ	English Language & Literature, History	INTJ	Computer Science, Chemistry, Architect
ISTJ	Political Science, Public Policy	INTP	Astronomy, Physics, Law, Biology
ESFP	Journalism, Media Communication	ENTP	Philosophy, Linguistics, Advertising
ESFJ	Nursing, Sociology, Teacher	ENTJ	Political Science, International Relations

1. **apply yourself** To focus and try hard. *I'm going to apply myself this semester and make straight A's.*
2. **clique** a small group of like-minded people. *She's in the cheerleader clique. I don't like their cliquish behavior.*
3. **credits, hours** sometimes a three-hour class is worth only two credits. *I'm taking 18 hours, but only 16 credits.*
4. **deadbeat, freeloader** lazy person, who does not do their share. *He's a deadbeat. She's a freeloader.*
5. **drop-add period** usually the first two weeks of class when you can change courses. *When does drop add end?*
6. **dumb down** to grade a test or course easier, so that "dumber" students can make a better grade.
   The average class ability is lower than last year, so the professor dumbed down the course.
   I dumbed down on the placement test so that I would not get put in an advanced class.
7. **GPA** = grade point average In America, the top GPA is 4.0, in Korea it is 4.5. *How was your GPA last semester?*
8. **grade on a curve** The number of students who can make an A and B is limited.
   The syllabus said that the class will be graded on a curve: no more than 30% A, 35% B, and the rest 35%.
9. **plagiarize, plagiarism** to copy writing and pretend it's your own. *If you plagiarize, you'll make an F.*
   If you're caught plagiarizing, you'll fail the course. Our professor has zero tolerance for plagiarism.
10. **pull an all-nighter** to stay up all night studying. *I pulled an all-nighter. Will you pull an all-nighter before the test?*
11. **scholarship** money from the school, usually scholarship means free tuition. *Did you ever get a scholarship?*
12. **stay out, gap year** to stay out of school for a semester or a year, to rest, or to study to get into a better school.
    Did you ever stay out a year? I stayed out for a year and took the Soonung again. I took a gap year after my third year.
13. **zero tolerance** no forgiveness, no mercy. *This school has a zero tolerance policy for cheating.*

14. **commute** to travel a long distance to school or work *Do you commute? How long is your commute?*
15. **off campus** nearby, outside of campus. *You live in the dorm? On or off campus? I live off campus.*
16. **walking distance** close enough to walk to school, usually 5 or 10 minutes away. *I live within walking distance.*

COURSES

17. **major** = a course in your major
18. **double major**: majoring in two related fields
19. **required** = a course you must take
20. **elective** = anything you like
21. **minor**: a secondary field

YEAR

22. **freshman** = 1st year
23. **sophomore** = 2nd year
24. **junior** = 3rd year
25. **senior** = 4th year

He went to Harvard,
but works at a chicken place.
Which idiom best describes him?

There's also a Listening Quiz on page 124. Go.

ELEVATOR SPEECH

About my academic personality: I would love to be an ***idea person****, but I'm just not. I've always been a* ***detail person****. That's why I like coding so much. It's all details. And, I have a* ***long attention span****, so I can do coding for hours. Sometimes I work all night in our club room, below the auditorium. So, that does make me pretty* ***computer savvy****. I was an* ***overachiever*** *in high school, but that* ***burned me out****. I was mentally exhausted after I took the university entrance exam. I was not a* ***brainiac****, I just studied hard, and had no social life. I don't worry if a professor is an* ***easy*** *or* ***hard grader****. Most classes are* ***graded on a curve****, so, grading is pretty standard. Now at college, I tried to* ***cram*** *for exams, but that didn't work. My brain retains nothing when I am tired. The* ***bad news is****, my parents were* ***strict*** *about grades when I was in high school. The* ***good news is*** *that now they are more* ***lenient****. My father especially wants me to enjoy the college experience. My major and my club are about coequal. I realize the value of a good* ***GPA*** *to get a job, but the* ***connections*** *I make in college are also important.* 211 words

SUGGESTION

Read, record, and listen to your **Elevator Speech**. Several times. Better yet, watch it.

WHY?

In human history, nobody ever did anything great the first time. (Columbus missed Japan by a whole ocean.)

If you don't like the way you sound, ***how do you think your classmates feel?***

RELAX!

Essays and Presentations are not some big mysterious things.

They have 3 parts: Beginning, Middle, End

In other words: Introduction with 1, 2, 3 • 1, 2, 3 Paragraphs • Conclusion with 1, 2, 3

1 INTRODUCTION, with 1,2,3. (First, Second, Third)

HOOK The first sentence is usually the 'hook'. Something that hooks you, like a fish. It grabs you, gets your attention. It should be interesting and make you want to continue reading and wonder, *How will this story end?*

The first sentence might also be called 'background knowledge'. For example, if you're writing that your iPad is your most important tech device, you might begin with, *My iPad has saved my scholarship several times.*

TOPIC SENTENCE Therefore, your first sentence is not necessarily your topic sentence. The topic sentence tells you what the essay is about. *My iPad is my most important tech device, because of 1, 2, 3.*

2 1, 2, 3 PARAGRAPHS, with specific examples

These paragraphs give three reasons why your iPad is so important.

*First, I use it for **communication**. For example, Kakao, Facebook . . .*
*Second, I use it for **entertainment**. For example, YouTube, Netflix . . .*
*Third, I use it for **education**: Wikipedia, BBC . . .*

3 CONCLUSION, with 1,2,3

The conclusion is a mirror of the introduction.
You say the same thing (in the same order 1, 2, 3,) in different words. You might also go for a boffo ending (like a hook) and include an implication (possible effect) regarding the future: *Therefore, when the new iPads come out, I'll be first in line.*

Jade Kim

Are you an introvert or an extrovert?

Introduction

There is a saying: "Your clothes are your wings," but I think personality is more importan' " ... ors person, and a **weekend warrior**. I take after ... d he's in sales. My mother's personality is just the ... than my dad. So, in personality I take after my father, and in looks after my mother.

First

First, I'm a **joiner**. I love doing things with people. For example, I belong to two clubs: an English club and compute ... my major's soccer team. My compute ... glish because most computer terms are English. We work long hours at the computer club, but that's OK because I'm also a **detail person** with a **long attention span**.

Second

Second, I hate staying indoors. I'm an **outdoors person**. I can't study at home because there are too many **distracti** ... the library. When I'm at home ... I'm in jail. On Saturday mornings I go jogging, and in the afternoon and evening I meet my friends at Hyewha. Every Sunday after church our family goes mountain hiking and then eat out.

Third

Third, I like to party on the weekends. I'm a **weekend warrior**. During the week I study every night so that my weekend ... During the week I get stress, and on th ... stress. I meet my friends at BHC in Chongno. I am not a **foodie**, I eat anything. I'm a **party animal** this semester. I studied hard for 3 years in high school and I want my reward.

Conclusion

I may not be an average person, but I think that life is short and I want to have fun while I'm y ... around a lot of people. That is why I'm an **extrove** ... and a **weekend warrior**. A university is where you learn, and socialize. I plan on doing both. My motto is: *Let's do it.* 362 words

Why so much repetition?

1. Human nature. To remember something (like a phone number or address), you must use it several times.
2. A typical essay and presentation might contain 400 words. If one word idea is repeated 3 times, it must be important.
3. Repetition, A) lets you know what's important, and B) helps you remember it.

What are the 3 parts of most movies?

Boy meets girl, boy loses girl, boy gets girl.

There's more info on page 98

ESSAY

Are you an idea person or an detail person?

You can answer that question, or any below, or create your own question.

1. Do you have a long or short attention span?
2. Are you a bookworm or a slacker?
3. Why did you choose your major?
4. What is your most important course this semester?
5. What's more important, your major or your club?
6. Is your goal a scholarship? How will you get it?
7. A prodigy or just a hard-working high achiever?
8. What courses are you taking this semester?
9. What are your three most important courses?
10. Will you (or did you) take a gap year? Why?

INTRODUCTION I chose because

1. I love computer animation
2. Good job
3. Work from anywhere

1 Computer graphics

Idea and detail person
Long attention span
In demand in many fields

2 Get a good job

Job security
Big, prestige company
English is the common language

3 Work from anywhere

I hate commuting
More quality time
Office when necessary

CONCLUSION I chose because

1. I love computer graphics
2. Good job
3. Work from anywhere

Why did I choose my major?

After the university entrance exam, I faced a dilemma: Do I go to a university in Seoul with a major I do not like, or a university outside of Seoul with a major that I love? I chose a major I love, because passion always wins. My parents had long advised me to choose a **STEM** major, and that was my plan. I chose Computer Science and Technology. **First**, because **I love computer animation**. **Second**, I'm guaranteed **a good, high-paying job**. And **third**, I can **work from anywhere**, at home or any country.

First, I have always been interested in computer graphics. My great interest is programming software for computer games. I'm a rare combination of **idea person** and **detail person**, so this suits me perfectly. Gaming requires ideas, and the detailed **attention span** to carry them out. And, with the core skills, there's great flexibility. I could go into gaming, Bitcoin, finance, medical, media, you name it.

Second, because computer skills are in such demand, that I'm assured of a good, high-paying job. Job security, and financial security, are also important to me. My goal is to get a good job with a big company, such as Samsung, Kakao or YouTube and learn all that I can. Then start my own company, or maybe work **freelance**. Also, computer terminology is all in English, so this field will improve my English, which may also improve my pay.

Third, I could work from home, for at least some of the time. I absolutely hate commuting. I do not want to spend hours every day getting to and from work. The Covid pandemic showed that working from home is very doable. And, working from home gives more **quality time** with the family. Of course, initially, working in an office with a **mentor** and **soaking up** all the knowledge I can, could be a good experience.

My father said that ***"Life is a contest of passion, ability, and showing up on time."*** So I am going to follow my **passion in computers**. It's field that I can excel in. Also, it's a great field for getting a **good, high-paying job.** Computer tech people will always be in great demand. Finally, **working from home**, or anywhere in the world, is a great option. In sum, I like the **passion**, **financial security** and **freedom** that software programming promises. 394 words.

Computer graphics

Computer skills

Work from home, no subway

EXAMPLE: ***Why did I choose my major?***

Hook	*After the university entrance exam, I faced a dilemma.*
Topic Sentence	*I chose Computer Science and Technology.*
First	*I have always been interested in computer graphics.*
Second	*Computer skills are in such demand, that I'm assured of a high-paying job.*
Third	*I can work from anywhere, at home or any country.*

INTRODUCTION

Hook ______________________________

Topic Sentence ______________________________

First ______________________________

Second ______________________________

Third ______________________________

1 ______________________________

____

____

____

2 ______________________________

____

____

____

3 ______________________________

____

____

____

CONCLUSION

1. ______________________________
2. ______________________________
3. ______________________________

Plan B. **This topic would greatly increase your ability to talk about your courses in English.**

What courses are you taking this semester?

I'm a at Sejong majoring in Spanish. This semester I'm taking 6 courses, 18 hours. Two major courses, two courses, one course and one course. I'm taking **Spanish History, Spanish Grammar, Descriptive Writing, Business Math, Sports Dance** and **Web Design**.

1 Spanish History is my most important class. It's in the grad school building and it's a big class, there's about 45 students. Mr. Gonzalez is the professor and he's Spanish. He speaks only Spanish in class but after class he will sometimes explain things in English. We will have four small tests and two term papers instead of just a midterm and final. I hear that he's an **easy grader**, but I don't know yet.

2 Spanish Grammar. We cover grammar, which is just a lot of memorizing, which is not my strong point. The class is only an hour, once a week, so that is good for my **short attention span**. The class is large, about 100 students, so hopefully I'll make a lot of new friends who I can study with.

3 Descriptive Writing is my favorite class, but it's also the hardest. We have to write two papers every week. The goal is that we get good at writing clearly, and fast. Actually, one paper is descriptive and the other is an academic essay, describing the same thing. There is no peer editing, which I love, because I hate for classmates to read my writing.

4 Business Math is also hard. I may **drop** this course. The professor is from India and has a strong accent and it's just tiring to try to understand him. I took this class because I'm good in math and I thought I would get an easy A. But I heard he's a **hard grader**. My classmate told me not to drop, I would eventually get used to his accent.

5 Sports Dance class we have just once a week for three hours. Normally I would love this class but it starts at 9 a.m. All the other times were filled. I want to make sure I get enough exercise so I took this class. I had Sports Dance in high school so this class should be pretty easy. I hope I can bring my GPA up with this class.

6 Web Design is challenging. Very. I feel like a visitor to another planet. All the terms and everything are new to me. This class meets three times a week. The professor is a total nerd who is really into web design. However, he knows his stuff and he's very patient with explaining things. I hope this class will help me make better presentations in all my future classes. But, web design requires a lot of detail work, and I'm not a **detail person**.

That's my schedule: My busiest day is Monday, I have 4 courses back-to-back, so I have no time for lunch. My easiest day is Wednesday, I have only one course, and Friday is my free day. So far, so good.

503 words

You can download the MS Word Template from the website.

Connecting Words

Here are words that help connect thoughts, sentences, and paragraphs.

Good writing has variety. To save time when writing, some people simply use **and, and, and**, repeatedly. After finishing, they go through and alternate. They use: **and, also, in addition, further, moreover, furthermore**. And then start all over.

Likewise, when you need to change direction use **but**, then **however**, then **on the other hand**. And repeat. Variety.

TO PUT THINGS IN ORDER

First, Second, Third	***First***, *open download the template. Second, download it. Third, open it.*
Next, Then	***Next***, *delete the example text.* ***Then***, *write your essay.*
Finally	***Finally***, *email the essay to yourself and to your professor.*

KEEP GOING IN THE SAME DIRECTION

And, Also	*I am fluent in Korean* ***and*** *English.* ***Also***, *I can speak tourist French and Italian.*
In addition	***In addition***, *I can speak a little Chinese.*
Further	***Further***, *I also have good computer skills.*
Furthermore	***Furthermore***, *I have four years work experience.*
Moreover	***Moreover***, *I have two years experience in sales.*

CHANGE DIRECTIONS

But, However	*My father is strict* ***but*** *my mom is lenient.* ***However*** *they are both old school.*
On the other hand	***On the other hand***, *my mother is very tight with money.*
Although	***Although*** *my mom might gives me money, I never have to ask her.*
Even though	***Even though*** *I don't have any money now, I'm sure my dad will give me some soon.*
Nevertheless	***Nevertheless***, *my plan B is to borrow some from my sister.*
Unlike	***Unlike*** *mom or dad, my sister keeps track of how much money I borrow.*

GIVE AN EXAMPLE

Such as	*Korean musicians have become extremely popular worldwide,* ***such as*** *K-pop.*
For example	***For example***, *BTS was one of Time Magazines 100 most influential people in 2019.*
For instance	***For instance***, *Jeni of Blackpink was the face of Calvin Klein, and Coco Chanel in 2021.*

MAKE A POINT

Because	*You can't drink* ***because*** *you have to drive home.*
So	*You cannot drink,* ***so*** *you might as well stop complaining.*
Since	***Since*** *you're thirsty, you could drink some juice or cola.*
Thus	***Thus***, *you will not have to take the subway home.*
Therefore	***Therefore***, *you will not have to come back tomorrow to get your car.*
As a result	***As a result***, *you will not get arrested for drunken driving.*

MAKE A CONCLUSION

In sum	***In sum***, *after you make your outline, it's just a matter of filling in details.*
In conclusion	***In conclusion***, *the most important quality of a presentation is that it is interesting.*

PRAISE

LIFE TIP #2. The secret to success in life is sincerity. When you can fake that you've got it made.

The more compliments you give (real or fake), the more you will be liked. Life – and love – is like a mirror, you get back what you send out.

In this unit, lie and compliment, like you do to your grandparents before they give you money on Lunar New Year.

(And, don't give the exact same praise to every partner. Change it up. They may realize you are not sincere.)

LEE *Hi. I liked your presentation. It was **awesome**!*

KIM *Thanks a lot. But, really.*

LEE *Really. It was **great**. I liked everything about it.*

KIM *For example?*

LEE *I liked your topic. I think describing your schedule this semester is **a good way to go**.*

KIM *Thanks. I liked your topic, on why you chose your major. That's a great topic to be fluent in.*

LEE *And your slides were **superb**. The **colors worked well together**. Your transitions were **smooth and catchy**.*

KIM *Was the text OK, too big or too small?*

LEE *Your lettering was **great**. I liked that your fonts were **simple and easy to read**. My fonts were **too busy**, I think. I realized that after seeing your presentation.*

KIM *Yeah, fonts. I like to use **simple fonts**, and only a few. If you go with a lot of fonts and **decorative fonts**, it can **distract** from the presentation.*

LEE *And I think one of the **strongest points** of your presentation was how you **matched photos** to your courses. That's a **great way to add emphasis**.*

KIM *Yes, **emphasis** is important. You can add emphasis with a big font and colors, but also with your voice. And especially with animation. Like when the text **zooms in** from the left, or **explodes**.*

LEE *Oh, yeah, that was **excellent**, the way your last slide had fireworks. And your voice was **great. Natural, but enthusiastic**. It helped **pull me in and keep my attention**.*

KIM *Thanks. That's **very helpful**. I was worried that I was too monotone.*

LEE *No, it was great. And say, can you show me how to do slide transitions and text animation sometime?*

KIM *Sure, anytime. The more you compliment my presentation, the more I'll teach you.*

LEE *Deal.*

KIM ***I'm glad to help**. It's a law of the universe that the best way to learn something fully is to teach someone. So, helping you will also improve my skills.*

3 Are you tech savvy or tech so-so?

Prove it

PERSONALITY TEST ✓

1.	*Are you tech savvy*		or	*tech so-so?*	
2.	*Are you a Windows person*		or	*an Apple person?*	
3.	*Are you an idea person*		or	*a detail person?*	
4.	*Do you work on a desktop*		or	*laptop?*	
5.	*Do you use SNS (Kakao, Facebook etc.)*		or	*old school email?*	
6.	*Do you wear a smart watch*		or	*a normal watch?*	
7.	*Do you watch more TV*		or	*YouTube, OTT (Netflix, Apple TV)*	
8.	*Would you rather read a paper book*		or	*ebook & audio book?*	
9.	*Do you use smart pay (KaKao pay, etc.)*		or	*pay by check card, credit card?*	
10.	*Would you rather play sports*		or	*play a video game?*	

For example? What about you?

CONVERSATION 3

Good news, bad news • Yin and Yang

The solution to every problem creates a new problem

Lee *Hi. I really liked watching your video presentation. I can already tell that you are very* ***tech-savvy****.*

Kim *Thank you. That's very kind of you. I put a lot of work into it.*

Lee *Well it shows.*

Kim ***What about you?*** *Are you* ***tech savvy*** *or* ***tech so-so****?*

Lee *So-so. I just don't have the* ***attention span*** *for all that tech stuff. How did you get so good at tech?*

Kim *My father works for Samsung, and I always got his hand-me-downs.*

Lee ***For example?***

Kim ***First*** *his phones,* ***second****, his laptops,* ***third****, his fitness watches.*

Lee *Lucky you.*

Kim *Yeah, well* ***the bad news*** *is, I never get anything new! Are you Apple or Windows?*

Lee *Apple, all the way. MacBook, iPhone, and Apple Watch. The* ***good news*** *is my parents bought all that for me. The* ***bad news*** *is, now they expect me to make straight A's. My mom says "We did not buy you that stuff to text 200 times a day!"*

Kim *I know what you mean. Technology has a lot of advantages, but for every* ***Yin*** *there is a* ***Yang****.*

Lee ***For instance****?*

Kim ***First****, as you say, people can go overboard on texting. It's a black hole.* ***Second****, while there's lots of useful information on the web, there's also a lot of hate and misinformation, and downright lies. And* ***third****, there's porn and graphic violence.*

Lee *So true. Everything is good if you use it, everything can be bad if you abuse it.*

Kim *That's pretty deep. You may not be* ***tech savvy****, but* ***on the other hand*** *you understand the universe.*

Lee *Thanks. I read a lot. Books, not Internet. Say, have you chosen a topic for your presentation yet?*

Kim *Not yet, I like to get through the whole unit before deciding.* ***What about you?***

Lee *I think I'll do my presentation on the Internet's* ***Yin and Yang****. That topic naturally requires using a lot of tech vocabulary, which we need to use in our Elevator Speech. Kill two birds with one stone. What programs did you use?*

Kim *I use Word to write my essay, then I just copied and pasted on to Powerpoint. And narrate and record the video.*

Lee *How many takes did it take? Ha.*

Kim *About 10. Like professor said: "To get good at something, you do it more than once."*

This is known as the "lame excuse" look.

The good news is, his presentation came out great.
The bad news is, he forgot to upload it.

Write what you will say

Get smoother at the basics

If you can't answer the first easy question smoothly, no one will ask you a second question.

1 **What kind of phone do you have? How old is it? How many hours a day do you spend on your phone?**
I have an iPhone 14, it's almost new. I spend too much time on my phone, maybe three hours a day. It's an addiction.

2 **Do you have a Facebook page? How much time do you spend on Facebook per day? Per week?**
Yes, I have a Facebook page. I spend about an hour a day there.

3 **What program is the center of your social activity? How do you communicate with the world?**
I mainly use SNS, like Kakao, WhatsApp and Twitter. I belong to a Twitter group. That's how I stay in touch.

4 **Do you do your assignments on a laptop or desktop? Do you bring a laptop to school?**
Desktop. I'm a visual person, I like to see things big. It's easier to see mistakes.

5 **Are your parents tech savvy?**
Yes. Overall, my father is more tech savvy, but my mother is great for shopping and vacations.

6 **Did you ever send a text that you regret? Did you ever drunk text someone?**
I never did. But I used to get strange texts after midnight sometimes from my ex-boyfriend.

7 **What programs or apps are the most important in your major?**
My major is Business, so we use presentation programs, such as Powerpoint, Keynote and Visme.

8 **What will be your next tech purchase? What's on your wish list?**
I want to get an iPad Air with the attachable keyboard. And a stylus. Then I should be set for school.

For example? What about you?

Talk about what you wrote 3

Answer longer, in academic format, with specific details

Who, where, when, why, how, how often, how long, how many, what time?

1 **Are you tech savvy or tech so-so? Are you Apple or Windows? Do you like dogs or cats?**
*I'm tech savvy. However, my parents are not, and so I'm kind of like a technology translator for them. **First**, I'm Apple. I have an Apple Watch, iPhone, iPad, and 24 inch iMac. **Second**, I use a lot of social apps, for example Kakao, Facebook, TikTok and Twitter. **Third**, I don't know a lot of programs, but I am very good at the basics. Word, Excel, Keynote.*

____

____

____

2 **What computer programs are you expert in? What program would you like to be expert in?**
I'm proficient at Word and Excel. I'm not an expert, but what I do know, I know well. Next I want to master Keynote, Audacity and iMovie so that I can make presentations for class. I want to master making animated text for my presentations. Then, I want to learn how to edit videos in iMovie.

____

____

____

3 **What apps do you use the most? What websites do you visit the most?**
*__First__, I spend way too much time on Kakao Talk and TikTok. If I used that time for studying, I would have a scholarship. **Second**, I watch a lot of Netflix, but only because my parents pay. **Third**, I watch a lot of YouTube. I used to read books, but watching short videos is addictive. The bad news is, I now have an attention span of 3 minutes.*

____

____

____

Where When Why Who How How often

3 IDIOM OPPOSITES

1. **tech savvy** smart and knowledgeable. *He's very tech savvy. She's a slacker, but a tech savvy slacker.*
   tech so-so average knowledgeable. *Our professor is old school. He's tech so-so, but he tries.*
2. **long attention span** can concentrate for a long time. *I have a long attention span, I can study for about 4 hours.*
   short attention span cannot concentrate for a long time. *I have a short attention span. I get distracted easily.*
3. **drunk text, drunk dial** to text or call someone after drinking. Usually a bad idea. *I got a drunk text from my ex-boyfriend.*
4. **ghost** to go silent, to stop communicating *After I asked her to pay for lunch she ghosted me. I got ghosted.*
5. **intuitive** easily understand, natural, logical. *I like their icons, they're very intuitive. For example, the trash can is to delete.*
6. **user-friendly** easy to use. *I like iPhones because they're user-friendly.*

There's not a lot of TECH Personality Opposites, so here are a bunch of Tech Terms.
You know most of them, and some of them can jog your memory.

NFO SITES

1. Wikipedia.com
2. imdb.com
3. azlyrics.com
4. images.google.com
5. translate.google.com

FORMATTING TERMS

6. format
7. font, typeface
8. margins
9. spacing (vertical)
10. header, footer
11. indent
12. page size: A4, US Letter

PROGRAMS

13. MS Word, Excel, Powerpoint
14. Pages, Numbers, Keynote
15. Illustrator
16. Photoshop
17. InDesign
18. Audacity
19. Prezi

BROWSERS

20. Chrome
21. Edge
22. Explorer
23. Firefox
24. Opera
25. Safari

SOCIAL MEDIA APPS

26. Facebook
27. Instagram
28. Kakao Talk
29. Linkedin
30. Messenger
31. Pinterest
32. QQ
33. Quora
34. Reddit
35. Snapchat
36. Telegram
37. TikTok
38. Tinder
39. Threads
40. Twitter
41. WeChat
42. WhatsApp

Excuses by MBTI Type

ISFP *We had homework?*
ISTP *Check again. I handed it in.*

ESTP *No excuses. It will never happen again.*
ESTJ *My printer was out of ink.*

ISFJ *My dog ate my homework.*
ISTJ *I didn't know. I was absent last week.*

ESFP *Oh, you're my favorite professor!*
ESFJ *I gave you chocolate on Teacher's Day!*

INFJ *The line at the copy shop was too long.*
INFP *I think you give too much homework.*

INTJ *Can I bring it by your office after class?*
INTP *Oops. I was supposed to print it out?*

ENTP *Your tie matches your shirt very well.*
ENTJ *This is a conspiracy to lower my grade.*

ENFP *I was dropped on my head as a child.*
ENFJ *My bad. It won't happen again.*

MEDIA SITES

43. Apple TV
44. Disney
45. HBO Max
46. Netflix
47. Reddit
48. Spotify
49. YouTube

DEVICE

50. Adaptor
51. AI Speaker
52. Bluetooth
53. Cloud
54. Desktop
55. Dongle (British)
56. External SSD Drive
57. Flash drive
58. GPS
59. IoT
60. Laptop
61. Memory stick
62. Modem
63. Pad
64. Phone
65. Tablet
66. Watch
67. Wireless

WHATEVER

68. CCTV
69. Nanny cam
70. WiFi, Hotspot
71. Icon
72. SNS
73. Spam
74. USB, USB-C
75. cloud

PEOPLE

76. Blogger
77. Follower
78. Hacker
79. Influencer
80. Malicious comment
81. Netizen
82. Subscriber
83. Videographer
84. Vlogger

VIDEO EDITING

85. Clipify
86. Cyberlink Director
87. DaVinci Resolve
88. iMovie
89. Movavi
90. MovieStudio
91. Openshot Adobe Premier
92. VideoProc
93. Wondershare

MUSIC

94. Apple Music
95. Pandora
96. Shazam
97. Spotify

That's our 500th text today!

What idiom do these photos refer to?

I sent you what last night at 3am?

ELEVATOR SPEECH

Let's see, my tech life. First, devices. I'm an ***Apple*** *guy. I have an* ***iPhone 14 Pro Max, Apple Watch****, an* ***iPad Air*** *and a* ***Mac Mini*** *at home with a 32 in Samsung* ***monitor****. In addition to the usual, I make videos with my phone. I use the* ***iPad*** *when* ***commuting*** *to school and for working at school. I use the* ***Apple Watch*** *for health. It's great for* ***monitoring*** *exercise and sleeping. And the power of the* ***MacMini*** *with the big monitor is great for doing homework and watching movies. For* ***SNS****, I'm a simple guy. I mainly use* ***Kakao****, mostly to stay in touch. I use* ***Facebook*** *a lot, because that's how students in my major stay connected. I get my basic information from* ***Wikipedia****, and watch movies on* ***Netflix*** *and music videos on* ***YouTube****. Finally, for programs, I use* ***InDesign*** *for artwork and* ***Keynote*** *and* ***iMovie*** *for presentations. This is where my big* ***monitor*** *comes in really handy. I want my second major to be in Media Communications, and those programs and skills should really help. For my next tech purchase I want to get an* ***AI Speaker****, so I can search for information while I'm watching TV.* 204 words

___

___

___

___

___

___

___

___

___

___

Record, watch, correct, repeat

Did you know?

The average Korean university student spends an average of 2 hours per day on their phone.

The speech on this pages is 1.5 minutes long.

Which means, you could practice your speech 10 times in less than 20 minutes.

This is a new century with new technology. Use it.

There are basically 3 types of Essays and Presentations

1	**Persuasive**	*You should hire me because of my education, skills, and experience.*
2	**Good news, bad news**	*Electric cars are good. However, making car batteries causes pollution.*
3	**Informative**	*This semester I'm taking 6 courses, 2 major, 3 required, and 1 elective.*
	Instructions	*This presentation will show you how to make a presentation, in 5 easy steps.*

1 5-Paragraph, TOEFL, Thesis, Persuasive Essay

- It has: Intro, 1, 2, 3, (or ABC), Conclusion
- Indented paragraphs and transition sentences

2 Good news - Bad news • Pros & Cons • Advantages & Disadvantages • Virtues & Vices

- Has 2 parts, each part has 1 - 3 paragraphs
- Paragraphs are indented, sometimes with transition sentences between paragraphs

3 Information and Instructions

- Has 6 to 8 Paragraphs, and each paragraph is like a long bullet point.
- Paragraphs are not indented, and there are no transition sentences to link the paragraphs together.
- This format is common in Business, where the goal is to present as much information as possible, in a short amount of time.

1,2,3 Academic, Persuasive

Are you tech savvy or tech so-so?

Some days I feel like an interpreter for my parents. Not for language but for technology. They say that children's language acquisition and brain develop together. Well, I think that likewise, my brain and technology grew together. On the other hand, my parents grew up in the **stone age**, so to speak, and rely on me to explain tech to them. So yes, I am **tech savvy**. **In broad strokes**, I'll prove it by detailing, first, my **devices**, second my **social applications** and third my expertise in **programs**.

First, my **main tech devices** are my watch, phone, tablet, and desktop. My **Apple Watch** is great for monitoring health and exercise, and it's kind of like an extension of my **iPhone**. I get notices on my watch and I can even read my text messages on my phone. I use my **iPhone** for just about everything – social, school, surfing, entertainment. For details, doing assignments and watching movies, I use my **iPad**. I use my **iMac24** for presentations and movies.

Second, I'm really into **social apps**. My mother says that's a **black hole** and I have nothing to show for the hours I spend there. Anyway. I use **Kakao** with my friends and family, and most communication in my major and school are done on **Facebook** and **ITS Messenger**. I'm interested in politics and do a lot on **Twitter**. Because length is limited, it forces me to be **cogent**, so I like that **facet**.

Third, I don't know a lot of **programs,** but the ones that I know, I know well. I know that I'll be using **Word** and **Excel** for the rest of my life, so the sooner I master them the better. I watched a lot of tutorials on **YouTube**. There's a learning curve for **Powerpoint** and that took a while to master. I video record my presentations and then edit them on **iMovie**. When I make a **blooper** recording, instead of starting over, I can just keep going and edit in **iMovie**.

Of course, there's two sides to everything. My mother worries that all my tech is used too entertainment and not enough education. On the other hand, my father sees me as a free Apple Store Expert who can help him 24-7. **Tech devices** make my life more productive. I get more done in less time. **Social apps** enhance my life by enabling better and more contact with friends and family. Finally, **programs** help me make better assignments, faster. Tech is the future, and that's how I'm tech savvy. 415 words

1 

2 TALK

3

Good News, Bad News

What are the good and bad points of modern technology?

There's an old saying: ***Everything can be good if you use it, bad if you abuse it***. Modern technology is a great example of that. A good example of that is the internet and phones. A whole world of information is at our fingertips, and that information is not always correct. A good example of the Yin and Yang of information is that people can use their phones to mobilize people for government protests, and governments can track data to find the people who were protesting. As they say, it's a **double-edged sword**.

THE GOOD NEWS, about technology is that it's great for **communication**, **business**, **education** and **entertainment**. First communication. It's instant. There is much more collaboration in business and it's easy to keep everyone informed. Many industries such as banking, tourism and real estate have been transformed. Working from home is one of the great benefits. Also, everybody has a phone on them, and an added benefit is that people who are lost in a snowstorm or whatever, can be located. University degrees can be achieved totally online. Students can learn at home and discuss in class. Entertainment has been transformed. Music is downloaded instead of sold in stores. Movies and how they are viewed has been changed for ever. Instead of three or four major TV companies, there are many companies, such as Apple TV, HBO, Nexflix, Amazon, and even TikTok. It's a whole new world, and constantly changing.

THE BAD NEWS about communicating is that it can be tracked. Every email or text send leaves a paper trail. There is no wireless privacy. A very basic example that is a drunk text message. It's there forever. In business, knowledge can be so quickly spread that it can cause stocks to fall and banks to fail. And that might be based on good or false information. With so much knowledge available, many middle class jobs in the banking, insurance tourism and real estate have vanished. Those people must now find jobs. The new **AI Chatbot** technology has created all kinds of problems for higher education. All kinds of written assignments can be artificially made. This may fundamentally change higher education The **flip side** of education is the lies and fake news that can be instantly spread. Pornography has a whole new world of viewers, and porn producers.

Over Six hundred years ago, the printing press offered knowledge to the masses. It changed everything. However, all that knowledge led to religious wars that wracked Europe for over 100 years. Instead of uniting the people, the knowledge divided them. In the same way today, too many people are talking to each other in echo chambers. They're only communicating with like-minded people. As are their opponents. The result is that the world is turning into two radical camps, with little common ground in between. Modern technology is bringing out the best, and worst, in people. Instantly.

484 Words

Inform and Instruct

What courses are you taking this semester?

I'm a at Sejong majoring in Spanish. This semester I'm taking 6 courses, 18 hours. Two major courses, two courses, one course and one course. I'm taking **Spanish History, Spanish Grammar, Descriptive Writing, Business Math, Sports Dance** and **Web Design**.

1 Spanish History is my most important class. It's in the grad school building and it's a big class, there's about 45 students. Mr. Gonzalez is the professor and he's Spanish. He speaks only Spanish in class but after class he will sometimes explain things in English. We will have four small tests and two term papers instead of just a midterm and final. I hear that he's an **easy grader**, but I don't know yet.

2 Spanish Grammar. We cover grammar, which is just a lot of memorizing, which is not my strong point. The class is only an hour, once a week, so that is good for my **short attention span**. The class is large, about 100 students, so hopefully I'll make a lot of new friends who I can study with.

3 Descriptive Writing is my favorite class, but it's also the hardest. We have to write two papers every week. The goal is that we get good at writing clearly, and fast. Actually, one paper is descriptive and the other is an academic essay, describing the same thing. There is no peer editing, which I love, because I hate for classmates to read my writing.

4 Business Math is also hard. I may **drop** this course. The professor is from India and has a strong accent and it's just tiring to try to understand him. I took this class because I'm good in math and I thought I would get an easy A. But I heard he's a **hard grader**. My classmate told me not to drop, I would eventually get used to his accent.

5 Sports Dance class we have just once a week for three hours. Normally I would love this class but it starts at 9 a.m. All the other times were filled. I want to make sure I get enough exercise so I took this class. I had Sports Dance in high school so this class should be pretty easy. I hope I can bring my GPA up with this class.

6 Web Design is challenging. Very. I feel like a visitor to another planet. All the terms and everything are new to me. This class meets three times a week. The professor is a total nerd who is really into web design. However, he knows his stuff and he's very patient with explaining things. I hope this class will help me make better presentations in all my future classes. But, web design requires a lot of detail work, and I'm not a **detail person**.

That's my schedule: My busiest day is Monday, I have 4 courses back-to-back, so I have no time for lunch. My easiest day is Wednesday, I have only one course, and Friday is my free day. So far, so good.

Format, looks, are important. Be a detail person and format your essay correctly.

Does it look like it was prepared by someone who is proficient in English, or by a lazy middle school student?

Save your first, perfectly-formatted essay as a template, and use it to start off your next essays.

There's more info on page 100

ESSAY

This unit started with this question: ***Are you tech savvy or tech so-so?***

You can end it with this question. Or, you can answer any question in the unit. Or make up your own.

You are not just writing an Essay, you are formatting your Presentation and writing your transcript.

OUTLINE

INTRODUCTION:

A.S. for parents

1. Devices
2. Social apps
3. Programs

1 DEVICES

Watch
Phone
iPad, Mac 24

2 SOCIAL APPS

Kakao
Facebook
Twitter

3 PROGRAMS

Word, Excel
Powerpoint
iMovie

CONCLUSION:

Apple Expert:

1. Devices
2. Social apps
3. Programs

Are you tech savvy or tech so-so?

Some days I feel like an interpreter for my parents. Not for language but for technology. They say that children's language acquisition and brain develop together. Well, I think that likewise, my brain and technology grew together. On the other hand, my parents grew up in the **stone age**, so to speak, and rely on me to explain tech to them. So yes, I am **tech savvy**. **In broad strokes**, I'll prove it by detailing, first, my **devices**, second my **social applications** and third my expertise in **programs**.

First, my **main tech devices** are my watch, phone, tablet, and desktop. My **Apple Watch** is great for monitoring health and exercise, and it's kind of like an extension of my **iPhone**. I get notices on my watch and I can even read my text messages on my phone. I use my **iPhone** for just about everything – social, school, surfing, entertainment. For details, doing assignments and watching movies, I use my **iPad**. I use my **iMac24** for presentations and movies.

Second, I'm really into **social apps**. My mother says that's a **black hole** and I have nothing to show for the hours I spend there. Anyway. I use **Kakao** with my friends and family, and most communication in my major and school are done on **Facebook** and **ITS Messenger**. I'm interested in politics and do a lot on **Twitter**. Because length is limited, it forces me to be **cogent**, so I like that **facet**.

Third, I don't know a lot of **programs,** but the ones that I know, I know well. I know that I'll be using **Word** and **Excel** for the rest of my life, so the sooner I master them the better. I watched a lot of tutorials on **YouTube**. There's a learning curve for **Powerpoint** and that took a while to master. I video record my presentations and then edit them on **iMovie**. When I make a **blooper** recording, instead of starting over, I can just keep going and edit in **iMovie**.

Of course, there's two sides to everything. My mother worries that all my tech is used too entertainment and not enough education. On the other hand, my father sees me as a free Apple Store Expert who can help him 24-7. **Tech devices** make my life more productive. I get more done in less time. **Social apps** enhance my life by enabling better and more contact with friends and family. Finally, **programs** help me make better assignments, faster. Tech is the future, and that's how I'm tech savvy. 415 words

1

2 KAKAO TALK

3

OUTLINE 3

On a job interview, you will be asked about technology.

This presentation is your opportunity to impress people with your knowledge and skills in technology.

TOPICS

1. Are you tech savvy or tech so-so? Are you Apple or Windows? Give three reasons why.
2. Why did you choose your major? Why did you choose your minor or dual major?
3. What is your most important tech device? What are your three most important tech devices?
4. What is the most important program or application in your major? What are the three most important?
5. What are the good news, bad news, of technology? GPS? Phone cameras and videos? Nanny cams?
6. What apps do you use the most on a daily basis? Why?
7. Is your university, or major department, very high tech, or just average?

TITLE ______________________________

INTRODUCTION

Hook ______________________________

Topic Sentence ______________________________

1 ____________	**2** ____________	**3** ____________
a ____________	a ____________	a ____________
b ____________	b ____________	b ____________
c ____________	c ____________	c ____________

CONCLUSION

Result / Implication ______________________________

Are you a binge watcher?

Is that your mother dancing with Johnny Depp?

4 Types of Presentations

Narrated video

No memorizing. Focus on your voice.

Live, and recorded

Find an empty classroom, present and record

NARRATED VIDEO

- Read, record, and focus on your voice. Practice at least 10 times. Each time you will find, and fix mistakes.
- Record with Zoom, PowerPoint, Keynote or other. Include your talking head, or not.

LIVE, RECORDED

- Find an empty classroom and record yourself. Upload at school, or edit at home and then upload.
- If you are part of a team, your teammates can watch and make the presentation more realistic by asking questions.

LIVE, IN PERSON

- If you use your laptop or the podium computer, you can secretly read your notes, and look like a professional!
- Set up your phone and record, or have a classmate record. No matter what, your presentation should be recorded.

HALF & HALF

- For units 1, 2, 3, make a video. For your midterm test, you select your favorite, and present that in class.
- Likewise, for units 4, 5, 6, make a video, and then present your favorite in class for your final exam.
- Units 1, 2, 3 can be video, and units 4, 5, 6 can be in person. (First, improve your voice, then the whole package)

Narrated video presentations can be the final stage, or preparation for your live presentation.

Live audience, and recorded

Your teammates ask questions and give feedback

Live in class

Voice, face, body language. The whole package.

It's easy as 1, 2, 3

3 students of similar ability have a 17-minute conversation

Record it with your phone, and transcribe just what you said.

Download the example **MS Word** transcript template, and type just what you said. **MS Word** gives:
1 how many words you spoke, **2 how many times** you spoke, which gives your **3 average words per turn**.

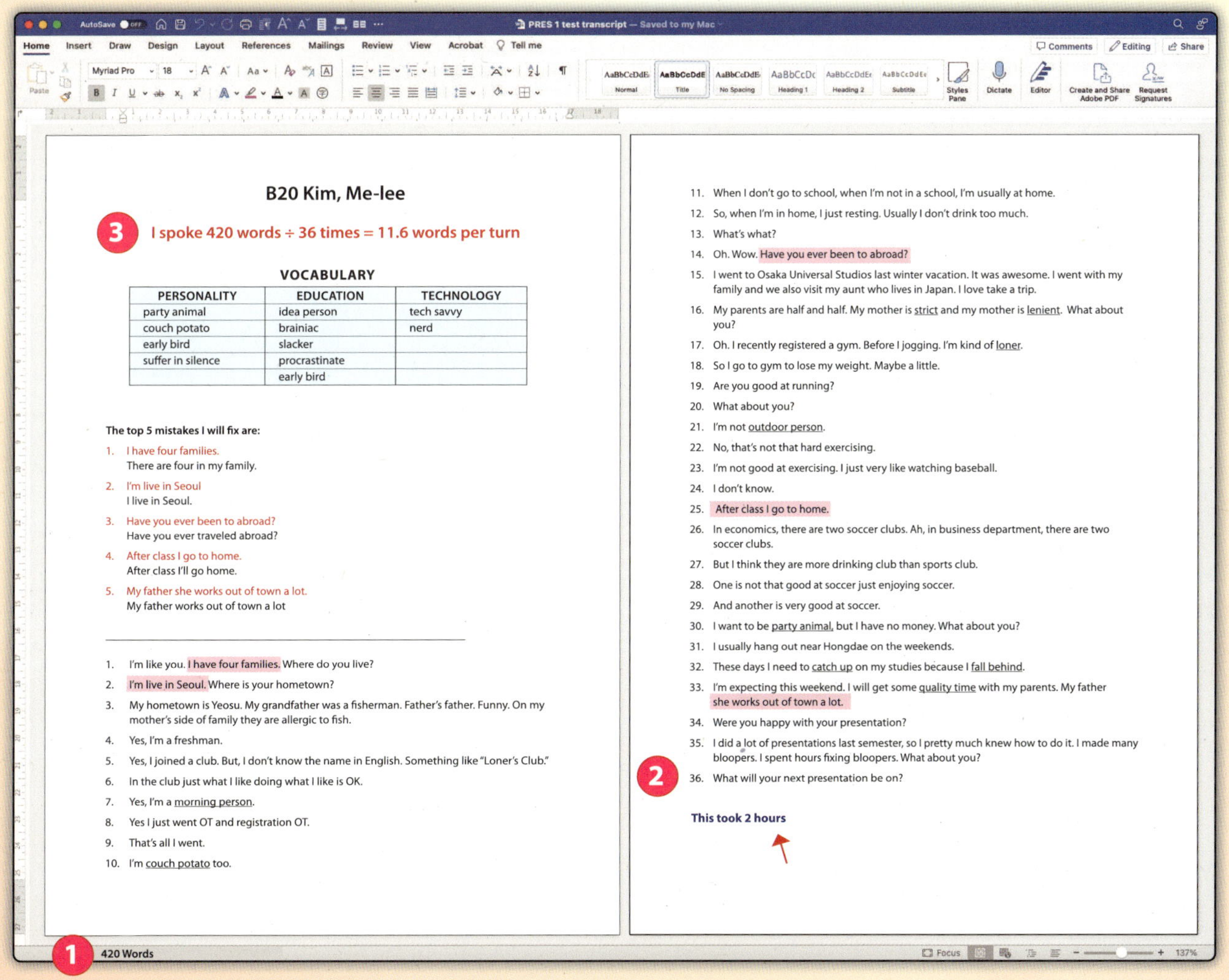

PRES 1 test transcript — Saved to my Mac

B20 Kim, Me-lee

3 I spoke 420 words ÷ 36 times = 11.6 words per turn

VOCABULARY

PERSONALITY	EDUCATION	TECHNOLOGY
party animal	idea person	tech savvy
couch potato	brainiac	nerd
early bird	slacker	
suffer in silence	procrastinate	
	early bird	

The top 5 mistakes I will fix are:

1. I have four families.
   There are four in my family.
2. I'm live in Seoul
   I live in Seoul.
3. Have you ever been to abroad?
   Have you ever traveled abroad?
4. After class I go to home.
   After class I'll go home.
5. My father she works out of town a lot.
   My father works out of town a lot

---

1. I'm like you. I have four families. Where do you live?
2. I'm live in Seoul. Where is your hometown?
3. My hometown is Yeosu. My grandfather was a fisherman. Father's father. Funny. On my mother's side of family they are allergic to fish.
4. Yes, I'm a freshman.
5. Yes, I joined a club. But, I don't know the name in English. Something like "Loner's Club."
6. In the club just what I like doing what I like is OK.
7. Yes, I'm a morning person.
8. Yes I just went OT and registration OT.
9. That's all I went.
10. I'm couch potato too.
11. When I don't go to school, when I'm not in a school, I'm usually at home.
12. So, when I'm in home, I just resting. Usually I don't drink too much.
13. What's what?
14. Oh. Wow. Have you ever been to abroad?
15. I went to Osaka Universal Studios last winter vacation. It was awesome. I went with my family and we also visit my aunt who lives in Japan. I love take a trip.
16. My parents are half and half. My mother is strict and my mother is lenient. What about you?
17. Oh. I recently registered a gym. Before I jogging. I'm kind of loner.
18. So I go to gym to lose my weight. Maybe a little.
19. Are you good at running?
20. What about you?
21. I'm not outdoor person.
22. No, that's not that hard exercising.
23. I'm not good at exercising. I just very like watching baseball.
24. I don't know.
25. After class I go to home.
26. In economics, there are two soccer clubs. Ah, in business department, there are two soccer clubs.
27. But I think they are more drinking club than sports club.
28. One is not that good at soccer just enjoying soccer.
29. And another is very good at soccer.
30. I want to be party animal, but I have no money. What about you?
31. I usually hang out near Hongdae on the weekends.
32. These days I need to catch up on my studies because I fall behind.
33. I'm expecting this weekend. I will get some quality time with my parents. My father she works out of town a lot.
34. Were you happy with your presentation?
35. I did a lot of presentations last semester, so I pretty much knew how to do it. I made many bloopers. I spent hours fixing bloopers. What about you?
36. What will your next presentation be on? (2)

This took 2 hours

1 420 Words

All this in 2 hours. So easy.

4 Do you believe in love at first sight?

PERSONALITY TEST ✓

1.	*Do you believe in love at first sight*	☐	*or true love takes time?*	☐
2.	*Do you forgive and forget*	☐	*or hold a grudge?*	☐
3.	*Is your boy / girlfriend high maintenance*	☐	*or low maintenance?*	☐
4.	*Is your boy / girlfriend touchy-feely*	☐	*or a cold fish?*	☐
5.	*Can you keep a secret*	☐	*or do you like to gossip?*	☐
6.	*Are you trusting*	☐	*or the jealous type?*	☐
7.	*MALES: Do you want a femme fatale*	☐	*or girl-next-door type?*	☐
8.	*FEMALES: Do you prefer: the macho type,*	☐	*bad boy,* ☐ *or a nice guy?*	☐
9.	*Did you ever lead someone on?*	*Yes* ☐ *No* ☐	*Were you ever led on?*	☐ ☐
10.	*Have you ever been stood up?*	*Yes* ☐ *No* ☐	*Did you ever stand anyone up?*	☐ ☐
11.	*Did you ever ghost anyone?*	*Yes* ☐ *No* ☐	*Were you ever ghosted?*	☐ ☐
12.	*Did you ever have a crush?*	*Yes* ☐ *No* ☐	*Were you ever crushed?*	☐ ☐

For example? What about you?

CONVERSATION 4

Love is like a mirror. You can only take, the amount you make.

Lee *Hi. How was your weekend? Hot date?*

Kim *I wish. What about you?*

Lee *I stayed home and tried to* ***catch up on*** *my homework. So, do you believe in* ***love at first sight****?*

Kim *Absolutely. I fall in love at first sight all the time. It's just always* ***one-sided****. What about you?*

Lee *Well, there's two schools of thought.* ***First****, attraction is primarily physical, which keeps you together until the mental attraction grows.*

Kim *OK.*

Lee ***The second way is****, mental attraction keeps people together until they feel comfortable with the physical.*

Kim *I think men are attracted to physical beauty, while women are attracted to financial security.*

Lee *Hmm. I* ***agree*** *about men, but I think these days with women working, they are less concerned with financial security. They can get that without relying on men.*

Kim *I'll go along with that. Do you* ***forgive and forget****, or* ***hold a grudge****?*

Lee *I can't stay mad long.* ***Forgive and forget****. And you?*

Kim *I'm just the* ***opposite****. I* ***hold a grudge****. I hate for a long time. I'm still mad at someone from the fourth grade. What are the most important qualities in your Mr. Right: looks, height, body, money, personality?*

Lee *I want them all. My friends tell me I'm too* ***picky****. If I can't have the perfect partner, I'll be happy alone. What about you? Do you want the sexy cheerleader,* ***femme fatale****, or the* ***girl-next-door type****?*

Kim *Oh, like most guys, I want the* ***femme fatale****. But my older brother told me "the prettier the rose, the sharper the thorns."*

Lee ***Yin and Yang****.*

Kim *Yeah, that's it.*

Lee *My mother told me to observe how a guy treats the waitress. If he's rude or unkind to the waitress, pretty soon he will treat you that way. Say, your last girlfriend, was she* ***high or low maintenance****?*

Kim ***High maintenance****. Too high.*

Lee *For example?*

Kim ***First****, she wanted about 200 texts a day.* ***Second****, she hated to be alone. I had to entertain her all Saturday and Sunday. And* ***third****, she was expensive. She liked trendy, expensive restaurants. Basically, she was* ***all take and no give****.*

Lee *Well, there's your presentation. You persuaded me that she was high maintenance.*

Write what you will say

Get smoother at the basics

If you can't answer the first easy question smoothly, no one will ask you a second question.

1 **Did you meet anybody special last weekend? Love at first sight? Eye contact?**
Not last weekend, but during orientation I helped a girl find a book in the library. She said I looked 'smart'.

2 **Do you believe in love at first sight? How long does it take?**
I believe. However it's important to stay within your league. Ever notice how many husbands and wives look alike?

3 **Did you ever have a crush on someone? How did it turn out?**
*When I was in middle school I **had a crush on** my tutor. He did a good job of pretending not to notice.*

4 **Were you ever discriminated against because of your gender?**
Yes. I had to go in the Army just because I'm male. I lost two of the best years of my life.

5 **Would you ever date a foreigner? Would your parents let you? Your grandparents?**
I might hang out with a foreigner, but I doubt I would seriously date a foreigner. Too many complications.

6 **How many blind dates did you have? How many first dates did you have? How many second dates?**
Let's see. I've been on two blind dates and about five first dates. Never had a second date. I'm very picky.

7 **What advice did your parents, or older siblings, give you about the opposite sex?**
My father advised me not to drink heavily around men. Never. With female friends, it's OK.

8 **Did somebody ever ask you out and you said no? Have you ever been turned down? Stood up?**
*Once in a coffee shop, the guy behind me tried to **chat me up** and asked me out, but he wasn't my type. I said no.*

For example? What about you?

Answer longer, in academic format, with specific details

Who, where, when, why, how, how often, how long, how many, what time?

1 **What are the top qualities you look for? Face, body, intelligence, height, personality, money?**

I can't lie, I'm a shallow guy. ***First*** *is face. There's an old song, "When my baby smiles at me, I go to Rio." When a beautiful woman smiles, like Jennie from Blackpink, it's like an addictive drug.* ***Second*** *is body, preferably tall.* ***Third*** *is intelligence. I think most beautiful women have the same basic aloof personality, that's why I choose intelligence over personality.*

2 **What's your type? Who are your top three movie stars of the opposite sex? That's usually an indicator.**

I like tall, slender, classy, dark hair, with an ***angular face****. Good cheekbones. Like Hyun Bin and Tom Hiddleston. I don't like* ***troubled*** *bad-boys. Troubled people spread troubles, my mother says. My boyfriend likes sexy blonds, like Scarlett Johansson and Jennifer Lawrence. He wants me to die my hair. If I do, I think I could find a better boyfriend.*

3 **Describe a typical date with your boyfriend / girlfriend. Do they offer to pay half?**

My boyfriend and I are foodies, so we like to eat out a lot. That can get expensive, but we're not much into clothes, and we're not big drinkers, so we save money there. We alternate between going to Hongdae, Hyewha and Kangnam. I offer to pay sometimes, but he never lets me. I don't know where he gets his money. I may have to check into that further.

Where When Why Who How How often

Femme fatale, high maintenance

Girl next door type, low maintenance

Idiom Opposites

1. **love at first sight** you love them the first time you see them. *It was love at first sight. We got married a week later.*
2. **forgive and forget** forgive easily. *Aw, he said he was sorry. Forgive and forget. Life is short.*
   hold a grudge stay mad a long time. *Are you still holding a grudge? I held a grudge against him for 5 years.*
3. **high maintenance** expensive to maintain, like a BMW. *She was high maintenance. She needed money and attention.*
   low maintenance easy to maintain. *She's low maintenance. I text her once a day, and see her once a week.*
4. **touchy-feely** a lot of touching. *He was too touchy-feely. Always holding my hand or putting his arm around me.*
   cold fish not physically affectionate. *She was a cold fish. We dated two months and never let me hold her hand.*
5. **keep a secret** to keep information private. *Don't tell her anything. She can't keep a secret.*
   blabbermouth, spill the beans to tell secrets. *He's a blabbermouth. He'll spill the beans. He spilled the beans.*
6. **trusting** they trust you. *She's very trusting. She trusts me. I used to trust him, until I checked his phone.*
   jealous, stalker possessive. *At first, he was just jealous. Then gradually he turned into a stalker.*
7. **femme fatale** sexy, seductive girl, like in the movies. *She's a femme fatale. Gorgeous, expensive, and lies a lot.*
   girl next door type nice, average, like your neighbor. *She's the girl-next-door type.*
8. **macho** manly man. *He's macho. He's the macho type. He acts macho in public, but he's just a pussycat.*
   bad boy a little dangerous, rebellious. *She's attracted to bad boys. She likes the bad boy type.*
   nice guy nice guy. *He's a nice guy. • She has low self-esteem. She's not attracted to nice guys.*
   pretty boy good looking, almost pretty. Like in a boy band. *He's a pretty boy. And always well dressed.*
9. **lead somebody on** to pretend to like someone. *She led me on. She's leading him on to copy his homework.*
10. **stood up** to promise to meet, then not show up. *She stood me up. Did you stand him up? Were you ever stood up?*
11. **ghost** to not reply to an email or text. *Will you ghost him? She ghosted me. Heck, I wanted to ghost her first.*
12. **have a crush on** really like someone. *She had a crush on her tutor in high school.*
    crushed VERY disappointed. *I was crushed when she said I was not her type.*
13. **wears the pants** is the boss. *Who wears the pants in your family, your father or mother?*
    henpecked male who is not the boss. *You are so henpecked! It's embarrassing. He's a henpecked husband.*
14. **toy boy** young male with an older woman. *She has a toy boy. He's a toy boy. Is that her son or a toy boy?*
    cougar older woman with a younger male. *She's rich and likes much younger men. She's a cougar.*
15. **gold digger** young woman who dates rich old man. *She's a gold digger. She doesn't love you. She loves your money.*
    sugar daddy old man who dates attractive young female. *That's not her father, that's her sugar daddy.*

MBTI Romance Types

ISFP	Believes in love at first sight	**ESTP**	Is high maintenance, and picky
ISTP	Is low maintenance, platonic friend	**ESTJ**	Nice guy, but a cheap date
ISFJ	Nice guy, but a mama's boy	**ESFP**	Bad boy, possible stalker
ISTJ	Most likely to get a Dear John letter	**ESFJ**	Might be a toy boy
INFJ	Likes the girl next door type	**ENFP**	Cannot keep a secret, gossip
INFP	Is always in puppy love	**ENFJ**	Dates around, does not commit
INTJ	Has too much baggage	**ENTP**	Charismatic, but plays hard to get
INTP	Tries to date out of their league	**ENTJ**	Macho, cold fish, likely to ghost

1. **admired from afar** you have a high opinion of them but were too shy to tell them. *I admired her from afar.*
2. **baggage** personal history and problems (such as drinking, drugs, debt, ex-wives, kids). *He had too much baggage.*
3. **blind date** a date with a stranger. *I had a blind date last weekend. I've had two blind dates in my life.*
4. **campus couple** a couple who go to the same school. *My parents were a campus couple.*
5. **cheap** doesn't want to spend money. *He was too cheap. His idea of a big date was kim-pab and soju.*
6. **cheap date** a low-maintenance female. *She was a cheap date. She was happy just walking and talking.*
7. **chemistry** to have mental attraction. *We like the same movies and music. We had good chemistry on our blind date.*
8. **charisma** mental attraction, charming, personality magnetism. *He has charisma. He's charismatic.*
9. **dating around** to date several people, one after another. *My mom told me to date around before going steady.*
10. **Dear John letter** a letter to end the relationship. *I got a Dear John letter when I was in the army.*
11. **drunk text, drunk dial** to text or call someone after drinking too much. *I drunk texted my ex girlfriend. My bad.*
12. **fix up, play cupid** to arrange a date *Can you fix me up with your friend? I fixed her up with my cousin.*
13. **love triangle** two men and one woman, or two women and one man. *Like in Titanic. It was a love triangle.*
14. **material girl** interested in material things, like money. *She's a material girl, give up. You don't even own a car.*
15. **Mama's boy** too dependent on his mother. *I thought he was Mr. Right until I realized he was a Mama's boy.*
16. **Mr. Right / Miss Right** the one who is right for you. *He's the one, Mr. Right. • I'm still searching for Miss Right.*
17. **nice personality** a polite way of saying someone is not attractive. *You'll like her, she has a nice personality.*
18. **out of your league** someone who is too good for you. *You're a nice guy, but that girl in the red dress is out of your league.*
19. **picky** hard to please. *She's too picky. She finds something wrong with every guy.*
20. **platonic friend, just a friend** you like them, but not romantically. *He's a platonic friend. He's just a friend.*
21. **play hard to get** to pretend you're not interested, to make them want you more. *Is that a firm 'No', or you're just playing hard to get?. • I played hard to get. • I played too hard to get, and he gave up.*
22. **puppy love** intense first love. *She's in puppy love. It's puppy love, you'll forget him next week.*
23. **the silent treatment** to not talk to someone you are mad at. *She gave me the silent treatment.*
24. **unrequited love** one-sided love, love that is unreturned. *It was a case of unrequited love. I adored her but she thought of me as just a friend.*

She's out of his league

The Listening Quiz is on page 100. Chop chop.

ELEVATOR SPEECH

Describe your ROMANTIC life. Or your wannabe romantic life. Or your parent's romance.

Pick a topic that let's you use the idioms.

In the old days, people would meet and decide if they like someone based on character. But these days, I think most people meet online, and the main deciding factor is looks and then height. Those are nice qualities, but they have nothing to do with good, long-term relationships. So far my romantic life at university has been so-so. I've been on a group ***blind date****, with three girls in my major, with four boys from another university. Never again, that is just too many people. It's like* ***herding cats****. I quickly decided that none of those boys were my* ***type****. My family is* ***affectionate****, but were' not overly* ***physical****. Those guys were just too* ***touchy-feely****. Then, one of my first cousins fixed me up on a regular blind date, and he was cute, but he had* ***prince disease****.* ***Stuck up****. He talked about himself all night. And, he was* ***rude*** *to the waitress, and that was a* ***deal breaker****. I gave him* ***the silent treatment*** *the rest of the evening. My cousin told me to* ***forgive and forget****, but I don't want to* ***lead him on****, so I* ***ghosted*** *him. Plus, he was* ***cheap****. If a guy cannot afford to pay for the date, he should not ask you out. Regardless, I think dating should shift back to meeting in person rather than surfing online.* 226 words

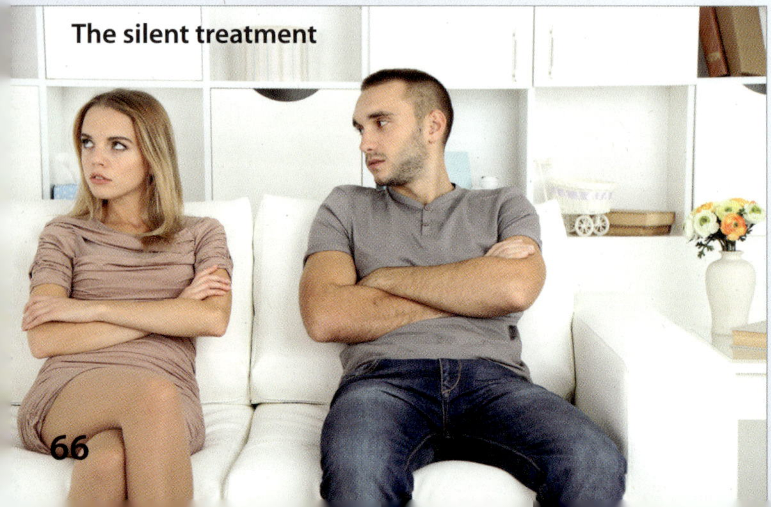

The silent treatment

Hold a grudge

Try to start your presentation like a *Mission Impossible* movie. *ACTION!*

Your presentation usually has the same (but shorter) introduction and conclusion as your Essay. However, you may want to punch up your Introduction and Conclusion. Below are some methods.

START A PRESENTATION

1. **Introduce yourself.** (Usually boring, so make it short)
   Hi. I'm an average, good looking, smart, multitalented university student with a great personality.
2. **Tell a story.** *When my mother was in college, female doctors were very rare.*
3. **Open with a hook, rhetorical question, interesting questions, statistic, chart, interesting fact.**
   Did you know that half of all university students are below average? But not me!
4. **Ask a 'what if' question.** *What if I got my dream job? Would I actually be able to do it?*
5. **Use a powerful quote.** Mark Twain said *"Eighty percent of all the things I worried about never happened." Therefore, I'm not going to worry about getting a job. I'm going to party at college.*
6. **Use a great visual.** For example, a photo of you skydiving, scuba diving, white-water rafting or bungee jumping.

END A PRESENTATION

1. **Your conclusion should be the twin of your introduction.**
   That's why you should hire me: my superior education, experience and ability.
2. **Use a powerful quote:** *Therefore, my motto for college is **carpe beerum**.* (Seize the beer.)
3. **State the implications.** *Being an intern will give me the skills, experience, and connections to get my dream job.*

There's more info on page 102

ESSAY

This unit started, and will now end, with this question.

Do you believe in love at first sight?

You can answer any question in the unit. Look them over.

Answer with persuasive TOEFL Essay and that will be the starter script of your Presentation.

OUTLINE

INTRODUCTION

I believe
1. Physical
2. Mental
3. Successful

1 Physical

Similar appearance
Body
Dislikes

2 Mental

Intelligence
Honest
Happy camper

3 Successful

Not necessarily rich
Dedicated
Money can't buy love

CONCLUSION

1. Physical
2. Mental
3. Successful

Love is a mirror:

Do you believe in love at first sight?

I do believe in love at first sight. Did you ever watch the home-buying show on HGTV? It's mostly married couples looking for a house to buy. Practically all of the couples look like they could be brother and sister. It seems obvious that people are attracted to people who look like themselves. And this physical resemblance can be seen at first sight. Now, of course it takes more than similar looks to have a great relationship. The other qualities that compose true love can be categorized into **physical**, **mental**, and **successful.**

First, I know it may seem **shallow** to say this, but **looks are important**. In general, tens marry tens, nines marry nines and so on.* Whenever you see a beautiful female with a **homely** male, the male is very rich. I'm into fitness and exercise and I do a lot to stay **in shape**. Healthy body, healthy mind, my mother says. I take pride in my appearance and I want my partner likewise. I could never be attracted to a **slovenly** or **dead-beat** looking person.

Second, mental. This covers a big range of qualities, such as **intelligence**, **sense of humor**, **personality**, **honesty**, **ambition**, and many more. Of all those qualities, the most important to me are **hard working**, **honest**, and **good manners**. I also want someone **confident**, with **high self-esteem**, and a **happy camper**. If you are not a basically happy person, I cannot save you. Unhappy people make those around them unhappy.

Third, successful. This does not necessarily mean financial success, although the two often go **hand-in-hand**. A successful banker will be rich, but probably not a successful carpenter. However, both have equal value to society, and have equal dedication and skills in their field. They just had different interests and education. Due to my parents hard work, I am financially secure, so money is not a top quality that I look for in a mate. Money can't buy my love.

In sum, I think that **looks are important** and this can be determined at first sight. Where do babies come from? Physical attraction. However, mere physical attraction is like a quick-drying glue – it also fails quickly. The other qualities that will make my glue last forever are **mental makeup**, and **success**. Finally, John Lennon said it well: *You can only take the love you make."* In other words. Love is a mirror. You get back what you send out. 406 words

Good looking

Happy

Successful

*This refers to 'a scale of 1 to 10'. 1 = awful, and 10 = awesome.

OUTLINE 4

TOPICS

1. What are the three most important qualities in a good boyfriend, girlfriend, husband, wife?
2. What is the most important quality in a boyfriend, girlfriend, husband, wife? And 3 reasons why.
3. What's more important in a husband or wife: mental or physical characteristics?
4. Is marriage necessary for a happy life? Are marriage and kids necessary?
5. If a man wants a chance at a second date, should he pay 100% on the first date?
6. Of the long, successful marriages in your family, what are three most important components?
7. Should couples live together instead of marrying? Live together before marrying?
8. Is marriage necessary or desirable in this day and age?
9. You could make a good new, bad news essay about your boyfriend / girlfriend's good and bad qualities.

You can use this presentation to clarify your own thinking about a mate. Or, this presentation can give you the opportunity to use and master a lot of the new vocabulary.

INTRODUCTION

Hook ______________________________

Topic Sentence ______________________________

1 ____________________
a ____________________
b ____________________
c ____________________

2 ____________________
a ____________________
b ____________________
c ____________________

3 ____________________
a ____________________
b ____________________
c ____________________

CONCLUSION

Result / Implication ______________________________

GOOD POINTS

Face	Personality
Body	Sense of humor
Looks	Dresses well
Height	Good family
Money	Good job
Brains	High class
Intelligence	Faithful
Education	Big spender

BAD POINTS

Smokes	Momma's boy
Drinks	Criminal in family
Curses	Low class
Gambles	Bad dancer
Poor	Bad grammar in texting
Lies	Always late
Unfaithful	Messy eater
Cheap	Chews with mouth open

BAGGAGE

Divorced
Kids
In debt
On probation

EXAMPLES, EVIDENCE, EMPHASIS

SPECIFIC EXAMPLES

Specific Examples are proof. They can be text, photos or videos.

Lee *One of the qualities I like in men is height.*
Kim *For example?*
Lee *My boyfriend is taller than me.*
Kim *So, you're not very tall.*
Lee *My boyfriend is 186 centimeters. Here's a photo.* →
Kim *You're right. He's tall.*
Lee *He's also very smart.*
Kim *For example?*
Lee *He says smart things.*
Kim *Oh yeah. Well, my sister is smart.*
Lee *Prove it. What is your proof, evidence, specific example?*
Kim *She scored 1600 on the SAT, and has a scholarship to Harvard, majoring in Artificial Intelligence.*
Lee *Got it. She's probably smarter than my boyfriend.*

EVIDENCE

SPECIFIC EXAMPLES are a very powerful tool in everyday life. For example:

You ask your father to buy you a new MacBook Pro. He says ***NO***. So you say:

Me *But daddy, if you buy me a MacBook, it could save you a lot of money.*
Dad *Really. For example?*
Me *First, I can do my homework faster and better.*
Second, that will get me better grades, and I can get a scholarship. And that will save you money.
Third, I can make a website for your business, and that will increase your business.
Dad *Hmmmn. Go get my credit card.*

ADD EMPHASIS with

1. **Text:** Make it **Big and bold.** Make it ***italic.*** **CAPITALIZE IT!** with an exclamation point. Make it **RED.**
2. **Slide transition**: A door opens, the slide changes color, or pops in.
3. **Type animation**: Text pops in or drops in, or zooms in from the side, or goes from small to big.
4. **Special Effects:** Fireworks, sparkles, start zooming.
5. **Audio:** Sound effects such as Applause, or a big bang.

CAUTION! If you emphasize everything, then nothing is emphasized.

ADD EMPHASIS with words, and voice.

This is important. • *This is **very** important.* • *This is **extremely** important.* • *This is **crucially** important.*

The words in red add importance. Or you can emphasis with just your voice:
Lower your voice tone, speak louder, slowly, and pause in between the words. **This. . . is. . . important.**

Another example. Sometimes, less is more.

Mom, I'm hungry. • *Mom, I'm very hungry.* • *Mom, I'm extremely hungry.* • *Mom, I'm starving.* • *Mom, **I'M HUNGRY!***

There's more info on page 104

Week 8: take the test, 17 minutes

Week 9: watch your test, 17 minutes

This is a new century with new technology. Transcribe what you said, and watch how you said it.

When you transcribe, you HEAR, TYPE and READ every mistake you made.

B20 Kim, Me-lee

I spoke 420 words ÷ 36 times = 11.6 words per turn

VOCABULARY

PERSONALITY	EDUCATION	TECHNOLOGY
party animal	idea person	tech savvy
couch potato	brainiac	nerd
early bird	slacker	
suffer in silence	procrastinate	
	early bird	

The top 5 mistakes I will fix are:

1. I have four families.
   There are four in my family.
2. I'm live in Seoul
   I live in Seoul.
3. Have you ever been to abroad?
   Have you ever traveled abroad?
4. After class I go to home.
   After class I'll go home.
5. My father she works out of town a lot.
   My father works out of town a lot

---

1. I'm like you. I have four families. Where do you live?
2. I'm live in Seoul. Where is your hometown?
3. My hometown is Yeosu. My grandfather was a fisherman. Father's father. Funny. On my mother's side of family they are allergic to fish.
4. Yes, I'm a freshman.
5. Yes, I joined a club. But, I don't know the name in English. Something like "Loner's Club."
6. In the club just what I like doing what I like is OK.
7. Yes, I'm a morning person.
8. Yes I just went OT and registration OT.
9. That's all I went.
10. I'm couch potato too.
11. When I don't go to school, when I'm not in a school, I'm usually at home.
12. So, when I'm in home, I just resting. Usually I don't drink too much.
13. What's what?
14. Oh. Wow. Have you ever been to abroad?
15. I went to Osaka Universal Studios last winter vacation. It was awesome. I went with my family and we also visit my aunt who lives in Japan. I love take a trip.
16. My parents are half and half. My mother is strict and my mother is lenient. What about you?
17. Oh. I recently registered a gym. Before I jogging. I'm kind of loner.
18. So I go to gym to lose my weight. Maybe a little.
19. Are you good at running?
20. What about you?
21. I'm not outdoor person.
22. No, that's not that hard exercising.
23. I'm not good at exercising. I just very like watching baseball.
24. I don't know.
25. After class I go to home.
26. In economics, there are two soccer clubs. Ah, in business department, there are two soccer clubs.
27. But I think they are more drinking club than sports club.
28. One is not that good at soccer just enjoying soccer.
29. And another is very good at soccer.
30. I want to be party animal, but I have no money. What about you?
31. I usually hang out near Hongdae on the weekends.
32. These days I need to catch up on my studies because I fall behind.
33. I'm expecting this weekend. I will get some quality time with my parents. My father she works out of town a lot.
34. Were you happy with your presentation?
35. I did a lot of presentations last semester, so I pretty much knew how to do it. I made many bloopers. I spent hours fixing bloopers. What about you?
36. What will your next presentation be on?

This took 2 hours

Taking, transcribing, and watching your test takes less than 3 hours

How much lifelong improvement does 3 hours of grammar study get you?

5 Are you a workaholic or a slacker?

PERSONALITY TEST ✓

1.	*Are you a workaholic*		*or*	*a slacker?*	
2.	*Are you a self-starter*		*or*	*do you watch the clock?*	
3.	*Are you a lone wolf*		*or*	*a team player?*	
4.	*Is your first impulse to spend*		*or*	*to save?*	
5.	*Would you prefer a high-pay, high-stress job*		*or*	*a low-pay, interesting job?*	
6.	*Would you prefer to work for a big company*		*or*	*work free-lance?*	
7.	*Pick one: job security and low pay*		*or*	*no security and high pay?*	
8.	*Pick one: house rich and cash poor*		*or*	*house poor and cash rich?*	
9.	*Is your father cheap*		*or*	*a big spender?*	
10.	*Is your mother a bargain shopper*		*or*	*impulse buyer?*	
11.	*On a team project, are you a deadbeat*		*or*	*do you do contribute the most?*	
12.	*Would you rather have: a nice house,*		*nice car,*		*or nice vacations?*

For example? What about you?

CONVERSATION 5

Lee *Howdy. So, are you a* ***workaholic*** *or a* ***slacker****? Wait, first: do you, or did you ever, have a part-time job?*

Kim *I work weekends at a 7-11 in my neighborhood? What about you?*

Lee *I worked full-time for a month at a cosmetics shop last winter vacation. So, are you a* ***workaholic*** *or a* ***slacker****?*

Kim ***Somewhere in between****. It's hard to be a* ***workaholic*** *at a 7-11. There's not a whole lot to do except to be polite.*

Lee *Did you like working there?*

Kim *I liked it. The pay wasn't much,* ***on the other hand****, I had a lot of free time to study. How did you like working in sales?*

Lee *I didn't care for it.* ***First****, I was on my feet in heels all day, and* ***second****, I found it tiring to be polite all the time. Now my co-worker, she was a real* ***people person****.*

Kim *Were you a* ***self-starter*** *or did you* ***watch the clock****?*

Lee *Oh, I* ***counted the minutes****, and when I wasn't busy I just people watched.*

Kim *The money you made last winter, did you* ***save it or spend it****?*

Lee *Oh, I spent it. As fast as I make it. I'm into* ***instant gratification****. What about you?* ***Spend or save****?*

Kim *I try to save at least half of what I make. My father gives me spending money, which helps me to save. And, the better my grades, the more spending money I get.*

Lee *Sounds like your father is training you like* ***Pavlov's dog****.*

Kim *Really. About the future. Would you prefer a* ***high-pay****,* ***high-stress job*** *or a* ***low-pay****,* ***low-stress job****?*

Lee *I might put up with a* ***high stress*** *job for a while, and then try to get in the slow lane with a* ***lower-pay, low-stress job*** *that I like. And you?*

Kim *I want money. I want the highest paying job I can get. I'm tired of* ***counting pennies****.*

Lee *Would you rather be* ***house rich or cash rich?***

Kim *House rich. I can stay home, have soju and chips, and watch a giant screen TV for entertainment. And you?*

Lee *I want to travel, see the world. Nice vacations, that's where my money will go. Any job that enables that,* ***I'm game****.*

High pay, high stress job

High pay, low stress job

Write what you will say

Get smoother at the basics

If you can't answer the first easy question smoothly, no one will ask you a second question.

1 **What's your dream job? What's your Plan B?**
My dream job is a TV and movie screenwriter. My Plan B is any job that is indoors and not blue collar.

2 **Are you the YOLO type, or will you plan for the future?**
I used to be YOLO, but heck, since everyone is living till they are 90, I want to plan ahead.

3 **Who's the boss in your family about money? Is your father cheap or a big spender?**
My mother handles the money, day to day. But my father is in charge of big ticket items. He's a big spender.

4 **How many jobs have you applied for? Were you ever fired from a job? Did you ever get a raise?**
I applied for a job at a movie theater to make popcorn, but they said I had no experience. To make popcorn!

5 **Is your goal FIRE, or a good, stable government job? Do you plan on being a DINK couple?**
I don't like FIRE. I think your occupation is a big part of your life, so even if you are financially secure, you should work.

6 **What's your next big purchase? Who will pay for it?**
I want to get a new iMac desktop. I do computer graphics and I really need it. For all tech, my parents pay half.

7 **Do you like instant gratification, or can you wait? Is your first impulse to save or to spend?**
I live for today. I like instant gratification. I hate to wait in line, like for a restaurant. I'll go somewhere else.

8 **How are you paying for college: parents, part-time job, student loans, scholarship?**
If I maintain an A average, my parents pay for all school, except for spending money. Tough love, I guess.

For example? What about you?

Talk about what you wrote

Answer longer, in academic format, with specific details

Who, where, when, why, how, how often, how long, how many, what time?

1 **Are you a workaholic or a slacker?**

*I'm a **workaholic**, it's **in my genes**. My grandfather is a farmer, and he works from sunup to sundown. **First**, I'm a morning person and I am never late. I'm early for every class. **Second**, I'm an **action addict**. I always have to be doing something, so I'm a hard worker. **Third**, my father taught me to never quit. I stay at a job until I finish.*

2 **Do you have a part-time job? Any kind of job?**

*My first part-time job was a math tutor. My student was a **slacker** and his grades went down so I got fired. Last semester I had part-time job at a 7-11 in my neighborhood. I worked on Saturday and Sunday, from noon to 8 pm. I worked for only one semester. The work was easy and the experience was good, but I had no social life, so I quit.*

3 **What does your father do? Exactly. What does your mother do, exactly?**

My father is a policeman, but not a traffic cop or anything. He works in the main office and he does background checks. My mother works for an online English education company. Specifically, they teach kindergarten age. She started off as a teacher, and now she teaches sometimes, but mainly she finds and trains teachers, and deals with parents.

DINK, YOLO

Material girls

Idiom Opposites

1. **workaholic** loves their work and works a lot. *My father's a workaholic. He works 70 hours a week.*
   slacker lazy, unmotivated, underachiever. *He's a slacker. He always does the bare minimum.*
2. **self-starter** if there's nothing to do, they find something. *She's a self-starter. She's always busy, never idle.*
   watch the clock just sits there, waiting for quitting time. *Stop watching the clock and do some work!*
3. **lone wolf** a loner, prefers working alone. *He's a lone wolf. He prefers working alone.*
   team player social person, works well in groups. *She's a team player, friendly and always willing to help.*
4. **people person** outgoing, extrovert, good with people. *He's a people person. He should run for student council.*
   anti-social introvert, prefers to be alone. *Stop being anti-social, you should go out more. Make some new friends.*
5. **happy camper** happy person (for example, even if the tent is leaking). *She's a happy camper. Always in a good mood.*
   unhappy camper, malcontent, moody not a happy person. *He's a malcontent. He's too moody, don't invite him.*
6. **house rich** most of your money is in your house, with little cash left over. *He's house rich, and drinks at home alone.*
   cash poor most of your money is in your house, car, clothes, or vacations. *She's house rich and cash poor.*
7. **company person** good, loyal worker. *He's a company man. He's worked for them for 30 years.*
   entrepreneur a French word, to start your own business. *She's an entrepreneur. That's her second start-up company.*
   freelance to work for whoever wants your services. *She works freelance. She's a freelance web designer.*
8. **suit** person with power, dresses well. *What does your father do? He's a suit at Samsung. Something in finance.*
   gofer lowest ranking assistant. Go for coffee. Go for = gofer. *He's not an assistant, he's just a gofer.*
   flunky lower than gofer! Flunked out of school, so has low job. *He's a flunky. He does flunky work.*
   grunt, grunt work hard, basic work, makes you grunt (Ugh). *He's not a suit, he's a grunt. He does grunt work.*
9. **instant gratification** you want it now! No waiting. Like a child. *He can't wait. He needs instant gratification.*
   delayed gratification mature, you can wait. *I can do delayed gratification. Good things come to those who wait.*
10. **share the credit, glory** mention the help of others. *She shared the credit with her team. She shared the glory.*
    steal the credit, glory to claim you did it all. *I did all the work and my partner stole the credit. She stole the glory.*
11. **white collar** office work, wearing a clean white shirt. *He's a white collar worker. He has a white collar job.*
    blue collar manual labor job. *He's a blue collar worker. He has a blue collar job.*

MBTI Jobs • Occupations • Careers

Type	Jobs	Type	Jobs
ISFP	Fashion Designer, Physical Therapist	**INFJ**	Human Resources, Mental Health Counselor
ISTP	Pilot, Economist, Civil Engineer	**INFP**	Graphic Designer, Writer, Psychologist
ESTP	Detective, Banker, Sports coach	**INTJ**	Investment Banker, Software Developer
ESTJ	Lawyer, Judge, Pharmacist	**INTP**	Architect, Economist, College Professor
ISFJ	Elementary School Teacher, Librarian	**ENTP**	Entrepreneur, Real Estate, Marketing
ISTJ	Accountant, Public Service Officer	**ENTJ**	Lawyer, Venture Capitalist, Executive
ESFP	Actor, Interior Designer, Children's Doctor	**ENFP**	Journalist, Advertising, Restauranteur
ESFJ	Nurse, Social Worker, Public Relations	**ENFJ**	Sales Manager, Human Resources

1. **DINK** Double Income, No Kids. *They're a DINK couple. We wanted to be a DINK couple, but SURPRISE!*
2. **FIRE** Financial Independence, Retire Early. *Work hard and save to retire early. My goal is FIRE.*
3. **YOLO** You Only Live Once. Enjoy life now, don't plan far ahead. *Let's go to Paris. YOLO. We can save later.*
4. **Trust fund baby** Has very rich parents, and will never have to work. *He's a trust fund baby.*

SHOPPING TERMS

5. **bait and switch** they promise something good, and give lower quality. *They tried the old bait and switch.*
6. **bargain shopper** waits to shop until there are bargains, to save money. *My mom's a bargain shopper.*
7. **big spender** likes to buy things, expensive things. *My father used to be a big spender. Mom stopped that.*
8. **champagne taste, beer budget** likes expensive things, but has little money. *I've got champagne taste, but a beer budget.*
9. **cheap** doesn't like to spend money, or only buys inexpensive things. *My boyfriend was cheap. Too cheap.*
10. **haggle** to negotiate and even argue over the price. *My mom likes to haggle. She's haggling right now.*
11. **impulse buyer** buys on impulse, without thinking. *I'm an impulse buyer. Why did I buy this hat? Sales people love me.*
12. **materialistic** interested in material things, money. *She was too materialistic. Only concerned with money and status.*
13. **rip off, ripped off** charged too much, cheated. *That place is a rip off. They ripped me off.*
14. **sticker shock** you are shocked at the high price. *I got sticker shock when I saw the price of that new monitor.*
15. **shopping spree** to buy a lot of things. *I went on a shopping spree with my graduation money.*
16. **shopaholic** loves to shop, addicted to shopping. *I'm admit it, I'm a shopaholic. Last weekend I was a shopaholic.*

CLUB BEHAVIOR

17. **clique** small group of people who think they are superior. *She's in the cheerleader clique.*
18. **deadbeat** someone who does not pay. Also, often a slacker. *He's a deadbeat, don't expect any help from him.*
19. **freeloader** does not contribute, rides for free. *She's a freeloader. She freeloaded off me. She freeloads on every project.*
20. **herding cats** it hard to train cats to act in a group. *Trying to get our club to do something is like herding cats.*
21. **prioritize** to place in order of importance. *You'll have to prioritize: your grades, your club, or your girlfriend.*

BUSINESS RANK

22. **entry level position** lowest position to be hired. *It's an entry level position, but I hope to move up soon.*
23. **intern** work for free for the experience, hoping you might be hired. *I was an intern at Google for a summer.*
24. **low man on the totem pole** lowest ranking person, most junior. *You're low man on the totem pole. Change the tire.*

Team players

She's not a team player

ELEVATOR SPEECH

About my working personality: I wouldn't say I'm a **workaholic**, *but I am a hard worker. I'm a* **self-starter**. *I would never* **watch the clock**, *that would be like stealing. My skill set includes the rare combination of* **idea person** *and* **detail person**. *I can* **think outside the box** *to find solutions, and I have a* **long attention span** *that comes with a* **detail person**. *Also, I'm a* **people person** *who's a good* **team player**, *but I can also work alone without close supervision. Tell me what to do, and I'll amaze you with how I do it. I would never* **badmouth** *my boss, I think that is* **low class.** *However, if there was anything illegal happening, I would definitely* **blow the whistle**. *I'm not risking my career to let some* **corrupt** *person get rich. Both my parents work for the government, so I know the importance of being* **above board** *and doing things* **by the book**. *My dream job is in advertising, and eventually I would like to start my own business. But first I would like to work for a big company for about five years to* **learn the ropes**. *I would* **learn while I earn**.

198 words

People person, self-starter

Watching the clock

The bigger your monitor, the easier it is to spot your mistakes.

The computer **microphone** is fine.
If your mom is buying you can get a $30 external mic.

The computer **camera** is fine,
or you can use your phone for better image quality.

Instead of spending hours trying to compose just the right amount of notes,
use slide presenter notes and spend that time improving your presentation, voice and speaking ability.

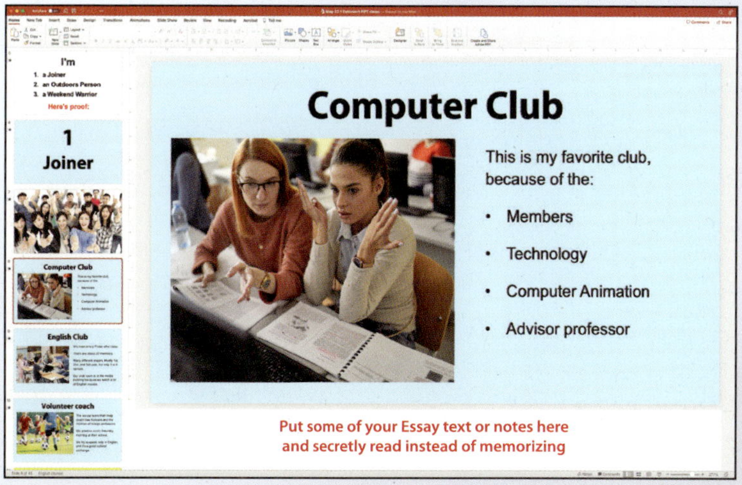

There's more info on page 106

Essay

If you know what company you would like to apply to, you can tailor this presentation to them.

For example if your dream job is at **LG Electronics**, make your presentation specifically for them.

And if you later apply to **Samsung** or **Google**, just change the name.

In general, when you submit a **statement of purpose** to a company, you could include:

1. Education
2. Work experience
3. Club experience, social activity
4. Goals
5. How you can help them

Are you a workaholic or a slacker?

Introduction
Hook
Topic sentence
1, 2, 3

Need you ask? Of course I'm a **workaholic**! I give new meaning to the word. And, there's more to me than just **sterling** work **ethic**. When you hire me you'll get the **whole package**: looks, brains, education, work experience, computer skills and people skills. I'll just **cut to the chase**. I've done my research on your company and I am the exact person that you need. Look no further.

1 **First**, my major and minor ensure that I have a rare and valuable **skill set**. My Computer Science major ensures that I am current with the latest, **cutting edge** technology. Technology is ever changing and practically has it's own language and you could say that I am bilingual in English and Technology. My minor in the Humanities – History – means that I can also put current technology and events into a **historical context**. Which, enables me to better anticipate the future.

2 **Second**, my job experience is very valuable. For three years, I worked-part time at the National Traffic Science Bureau. The research into traffic patterns was detailed, and required me to place all these **disparate** details into a **big picture**. This required a **detail person**, **idea person**, and **people person** who could sell our version of the big picture to **bean-counting bureaucrats**.

3 **Third**, my computer graphics and media skills enabled me to convert complex traffic data charts into easily-understandable Powerpoint and multimedia presentations. As Einstein said: "If you can't say it simply, you do not understand it well enough." I have the computer and coding skills to **crunch the numbers**, and illustrate the **trend** that the numbers mean.

4 **Fourth**, the first rule of sales is: "Knowledge and facts are good, but it's passion that sells." I have the persuasive people skills be an influencer, if you will. I'm a **team player** who realizes the value of building consensus, and then selling that consensus to management. That requires persuasion and consensus building. The fact that I was class leader in high school and university ensures that I have the popularity and responsibility to get things done.

Conclusion
1, 2, 3

There you have it. My **major and minor**, **part-time job experience**, **computer skills**, and **people skills** are the precise **skills set** that you need. I am not a **work in progress**. I am fully-formed, hard-working, creative, and persuasive. I bring all these qualities to you, if you just ***Show me the money!***

Reading history

Idea person

Detail person

Team player

TOPICS

1. What's your life philosophy: **YOLO, FIRE, DINK**?
2. Give 3 reasons why we should hire you. Give 3 reasons why we should let you into graduate school.
3. Is your first impulse to save or spend? Would you rather be house rich or cash rich?
4. Are you a team player or a lone wolf?
5. Is it better to work part-time or borrow money to pay for school?
6. Would you prefer a high-pay, high stress job, or a low-pay, interesting job?
7. What are the most important qualities of a good boss or company president? A good worker?
8. What corporate titan do you admire the most and why? Steve Jobs, Elon Musk, Bill Gates? Other?

INTRODUCTION

Hook ______________________________

Topic Sentence ______________________________

1 ______________	**2** ______________	**3** ______________
a ______________	a ______________	a ______________
b ______________	b ______________	b ______________
c ______________	c ______________	c ______________

CONCLUSION

Result / Implication ______________________________

High stress job

Low stress job

SHOW SOME RESPECT, DRESS NICE

Pull up your pants, stand up straight.

Show your passion. And tuck in your shirt.

DRESS NICE

It shows respect for yourself, and for your audience. Nobody wants to hear a bum speak. If you don't respect your appearance, why should other people? Your presentation might be so awesome that you can use it in your job application package. If your presentation is great, but your clothes are too casual, you will have to make the presentation again with better clothes.

EYE CONTACT

Make eye contact with as many in the audience as possible. Looking at the teacher every now and then is OK. But, do not present to the teacher. If you have friends in class, have them spread out. Then, when you make eye contact with them, you are looking all around the room, like a professional speaker. Ask them to look alert and smile at you. This will give you energy!

TECH

1.	**USB stick**	Bring your presentation on a USB and use the class computer.
2.	**Laptop**	Bring your laptop and connect it. MAKE SURE you have the right connections.
3.	**Clicker**	You can advance your slides using the wireless clicker. MAKE SURE the connections work.
4.	**Phone**	Record your presentation with your phone. It gives great feedback, and a permanent record.
5.	**Laser Pointer**	Do not use, it can make people confused and dizzy.
6.	**Microphone**	Not necessary. It's distracting. Speak louder, and assert yourself.

On her laptop, she can secretly read notes from her laptop, see which slide is next, and how much time she has left.

Maintain eye contact with the audience. Good posture is a big plus

SUGGESTIONS & GENTLE CRITIQUE

Here are areas that you could comment on:

ORGANIZATION: topic choice, interesting, well-organized, cohesive, persuasive, interesting

VOICE: Too fast, slow, high, low, timid. Emphasis, dramatic? Mumble? Articulate, pronunciation

TECH: Slides, text (too big, small, decorative), colors, transitions, animations, consistency

LEE *Hi. Of the presentations I had to watch, I liked yours the best.*

KIM *Thanks. But I heard you say that to your last partner.*

LEE *Sorry about that.*

KIM *That's OK, I appreciate your* ***white lies****. I can handle* ***constructive criticism****.* ***Gentle****, if possible. I really want to improve, and for that I need feedback.*

LEE *You got it. Honesty, but not 'brutal honesty.' First, I think your slides were* ***busy****. The text was small, and there was too much.*

KIM *How can I fix that? And you said "First?"*

LEE *Well, second, I* ***suggest*** *bigger text and less information on each slide. And, more contrast between the text and background color.* ***I found*** *your slide background was a little dark and the lettering was hard to read.*

KIM *I was trying to get* ***artsy****. But, with less text on each slide, I'll need more slides, and then my presentation will be too long.*

LEE *Yes, that's the eternal problem.* ***One thing you could do****: the slide transition times were long, a second or more.* ***I recommend*** *you use half a second. That would save you some time. And make that standard on your PPT template.*

KIM *Good idea.*

LEE *How was my voice, my delivery?*

KIM *To be honest, it didn't appear that you practiced many times. I think if you had* ***rehearsed*** *more, it would have been better.*

LEE ***Can you be more specific****?*

KIM *Your voice can be a very* ***powerful, dramatic instrument****. For example, when you said "This is crucial. . ." you said it in a normal tone. Add some emphasis:* ***This . . . is . . . CRUCIAL****. You can add emphasis with your voice, and with bigger text.* ***I suggest*** *using both. And red text can also add emphasis.*

LEE *Oh, that's good.* ***Would you mind****, next time, I'll send you my video before I upload it. Then I could* ***incorporate your feedback*** *into my presentation before I upload it.*

KIM *Sure, if you do the same for me.*

LEE *Great. But, you're much better than me at all this. I don't know how much help I can be.*

KIM *You can be great help, trust me. I'm an* ***idea guy****, not a* ***detail guy****, and there's so many little mistakes in my presentations that I don't notice. It's very hard to find your own mistakes.*

LEE *Yeah, I* ***noticed*** *you misspelled your own name on you last slide.*

KIM *Oh, that's embarrassing. See, you can be a great help.*

6 Are you a party animal or a party pooper?

PERSONALITY TEST

1. *Are you a: teetotaler* ☐ *social drinker* ☐ *weekend warrior* ☐ *binge drinker?* ☐
2. *Are you the life of the party* ☐ *or a wet blanket?* ☐
3. *Are you a party animal* ☐ *or a party pooper?* ☐
4. *Are you an early bird* ☐ *or a night owl?* ☐
5. *Are you a live wire* ☐ *or a stick in the mud?* ☐
6. *Do you have a high* ☐ *or low tolerance for alcohol?* ☐
7. *Are you an action addict* ☐ *or a couch potato?* ☐
8. *Do you suffer in silence* ☐ *or whine and complain?* ☐
9. *Are you happier alone* ☐ *or in a crowd?* ☐
10. *Are you spontaneous* ☐ *or you need advanced notice?* ☐
11. *Are you good at sports* ☐ *or the last one picked?* ☐
12. *What gives you stress: parents* ☐ *school* ☐ *money* ☐ *boy/girlfriend?* ☐

For example? What about you?

CONVERSATION 6

Lee *Hi. Are you ready for the weekend?*

Kim *Oh yeah, I have big plans. What will you do?*

Lee *Hit the road. Friday is my free day so I'm going to my hometown to see my parents.*

Kim *Nice. How often do you go see them?*

Lee *About every other weekend. What about you? On the weekends, are you an* **action addict** *or a* **couch potato***?*

Kim *Oh, I'm an* **action addict***. I'm always doing something.*

Lee *Ah, so you're a* **weekend warrior***. You behave and study during the week, and party all weekend.*

Kim *Yeah, that's me. School* **drains** *me, and socializing is how I* **recharge***. What do you in your hometown?*

Lee *Nothing. Just relax. I just* **chill out** *and* **recharge my batteries** *on the sofa. OK, so you're a* **party animal***. Are you a* **heavy drinker***? Do you have a* **high tolerance** *for alcohol?*

Kim *You could say I have a* **high tolerance***. What about you? Are you a* **social drinker** *or a* **teetotaler***?*

Lee *I'm a very light* **social drinker***. I have a* **low tolerance** *for alcohol. My face turns red. Are you a* **night owl***? Did you ever get home after sunrise?*

Kim *A few times. Party all night and sleep all day, that's me. Or used to be. I've got to* **buckle down** *and* **focus on** *my grades.*

Lee *Do you eat when you go out? Are you a* **foodie***?*

Kim *Maybe you don't know this: heavy drinkers are not* **picky eaters***.*

Lee *Ha. True. Where do you* **hang out** *on the weekends?*

Kim *Mostly around Hongdae, sometimes Hyewha. There's so much energy there, like electricity. Teeming masses of life.*

Lee ***I'm just the opposite****. Crowds like that* **drain** *me. Subways also. Bunches of stressed people. I much prefer the bus.*

Kim *Do you have a hobby, or ever exercise? Do you ever do something physical to relieve stress?*

Lee *I like jogging. I guess I'm a* **loner***. I just put on my earphones and go. I used to take ballet, and that was a good way to relax. I think that jogging is the* **best bang for the buck***. Highest number of calories in the shortest amount of time. Are you* **into** *sports?*

Kim *Yeah, but I like team sports, like soccer and basketball. I think a sports bar is a great invention. Sports and drinking! How can you beat that?*

Action addict

Couch potato

Write what you will say

Get smoother at the basics

If you can't answer the first easy question smoothly, no one will ask you a second question.

1 **Do you use the weekends to party, relax, catch up on your studies, or get ahead with your studies?**
During the week, it's all about school, the weekends are all about me. I relax and socialize with my friends.

2 **How often do you get the blues? How do you get back to your usual shiny, happy self?**
I'm a happy camper, I rarely get the blues. I got the blues when my boyfriend went in the army. I got over that quick.

3 **Does your personality change when you drink? Do you ever drink around your parents?**
It's funny. I don't drink much, but my friends do. And as their personality changes, I go along. So, yes. It changes.

4 **Are you talented at anything? Music, art, math, sports? Did you ever win a contest?**
I'm good at drawing and painting, most of my family are. I won a contest in middle school.

5 **What gives you stress: commuting, money, school, boy/girlfriend, lack of boy/girlfriend?**
Money. With more money I could have a better social life, and maybe find a girlfriend. Money would solve a lot.

6 **How do you relax? Doing something or nothing? How often do you get stressed?**
My father is big into family time. Once a month we go mountain hiking. And for relaxing I like to read biographies.

7 **How often do you exercise? Are you good at sports?**
I work out at the school weight room, usually twice a week. I'm pretty good at sports. I'm on my major soccer team.

8 **What's most important to you, your major or your club?**
To be honest, my club. My major is what allows me to come to college, but my passion is music and I love my guitar club.

For example? What about you?

Answer longer, in academic format, with specific details

Who, where, when, why, how, how often, how long, how many, what time?

1 **Are you an action addict or a couch potato?**

*I'm an **action addict**. I guess you could say both mentally and physically. **First**, on the weekends I'm **always on the go**. I'm never at home. **Second**, I love extreme sports, such as zipline, bungee jumping and white water rafting. **Third**, I like regular sports, especially soccer and basketball. I play soccer on my major club.*

___

___

___

2 **Would you like to take a gap year or hurry up and finish? What would you do during the gap year?**

One of the upperclassmen said that if you are not really sure what you want to do after your sophomore year, it's a good idea to take a gap year. Try to figure things out, so you can focus on your final two years. I'm in no hurry, I would like to take a gap year and travel to Japan. And maybe get a job and save some money so I don't need a part-time job while I finish.

___

___

___

3 **How many hours a week do you spend studying? Socializing? Drinking? Exercising? On your phone?**

I'm taking 18 hours of courses, and I spend about 2 hours a week studying for each class, so that's about 36 hours of studying per week. I socialize on Friday for about 4 hours, Saturday about 8. So, 12 hours socializing, which is one-third of my studying hours. I think that's a good ratio. I don't know how, but my phone tells me I spend about 3 hours a day on my phone.

___

___

___

Where When Why Who How How often

She's got the blues

They're having quality time

IDIOM OPPOSITES

1. **teetotaler** never drinks, never. *He's a teetotaler. He never drinks.*
2. **social drinker** drinks moderately, only to be social. *She's a social drinker. She drinks only to be social.*
3. **weekend warrior** is quiet during the week, but drinks heavily on the weekends. *He's a weekend warrior.*
4. **binge drinker** drinks rarely, but very much. *He's a binge drinker. Last weekend he woke up in the park.*
5. **life of the party** a very lively, and funny person, at a party. *She was the life of the party.*
6. **got a buzz** happy feeling after 2 quick beers. *Did you get a buzz? Oh, I got a buzz. I had a buzz.*
7. **wet blanket** a wet blanket puts out a fire. *Stop being a wet blanket. Have a drink! She was a wet blanket.*
8. **buzz kill** similar to wet blanket, but newer. *What a buzz kill. He's a buzz kill. He killed our buzz.*
9. **party animal** likes to stay out late and party. *He's a party animal. He rarely gets home before sunrise.*
10. **party pooper** pooped is slang for tired. *Opposite of party animal. It's only 8:00! Don't be a party pooper.*
11. **early bird** wakes up very early. *My father is an early bird. He gets up at 5, exercises, then goes to work.*
12. **night owl** goes to bed very late. *I'm a night owl. I start studying at midnight and go to bed about 4 am.*
13. **live wire** a live electrical wire will shock you. A very active, hyper person at a party. *He's a live wire. He never stops.*
14. **stick in the mud** a stick in the mud is hard to pull out. *Don't be a stick in the mud. Come have a beer with us.*
15. **high tolerance** can drink a lot, without much effect. *He has a high tolerance for alcohol.*
16. **holds their liquor** can drink a lot without much effect. *He can hold his liquor. He holds his liquor well.*
17. **low tolerance** a little alcohol affects them much. *She has a low tolerance for alcohol. One sip and she's buzzing.*
18. **lightweight** gets drunk after drinking only a little. *He's a lightweight. Two beers and he's drunk and sleepy.*
19. **happy drunk** gets happy when they drank. *Yeah, sure, invite your cousin. He's a happy drunk.*
20. **unhappy drunk** drinking makes them sad. *Don't invite him. He's an unhappy drunk, and gets in arguments.*
21. **suffer in silence** to endure, remain silent. *Do you suffer in silence? I suffered in silence, but I'll get revenge.*
22. **whine, complain** whine, complain *Stop whining. Stop complaining. Act like an adult, not a 2 year-old child.*
23. **spontaneous** does not need advance notice, ready for anything. *He's spontaneous. It was a spontaneous decision.*
24. **need advance notic**e you need time to decide. *Go out tonight? Not possible. I need advance notice.*
25. **social butterfly** a butterfly goes from flower to flower. *She's a social butterfly. Always on the go on the weekends.*
26. **homebody** likes to stay home. *She's a homebody. She likes to stay home on the weekends.*

MBTI Types at a Party

ISFP	Night owl, and really bad dancer
ISTP	Wet blanket, and designated driver
ESTP	Life of the party, spills drinks
ESTJ	High tolerance for alcohol
INFJ	Likes to console drunks, secret teetotaler
INFP	Unhappy drunk, tries to sing
ENFP	Happy drinker, big tipper
ENFJ	Buzz kill, complains about the service
ISFJ	Buzz kill, party pooper
ISTJ	Needs advance notice, likes to lip sync
ESFP	Social drinker, conservative dresser
ESFJ	Suffers in silence, stick in the mud
INTJ	Teetotaler, hangs out with the cat
INTP	Pigs out on dips and chips
ENTP	Wannabe Toy Boy, but too picky
ENTJ	Weekend warrior, organizes games

DRINKING: During & After

1. **dizzy** crazy feeling after you spin around three times. *That theme park ride made me dizzy.*
2. **faint / pass out / black out** lose consciousness. Females faint, men pass out and black out. *He blacked out.*
3. **hangover, hungover** feeling poorly the morning after drinking. *I'm hungover. I have a hangover.*
4. **woozy** almost fainting, unsteady on your feet. *I'm feeling woozy. No more soju for me. I need some fresh air.*

WEEKENDS

5. **burned out** very tired mentally, like from studying. *I'm burned out after midterms. I need a break.*
6. **catch up on** to catch up, to be current. *This weekend I'll catch up on my homework.*
7. **fall behind** to be late, not keep up with. *I partied too much last week and fell behind.*
8. **goof off** to be lazy, do nothing much. *I will goof off this weekend. I goofed off yesterday. I'm not goofing off.*
9. **hang out** to meet and do things. *Let's go hangout downtown and maybe catch a movie.*
10. **look forward to** to be happy about a future event. *Midterms are over. I'm looking forward to this weekend.*
11. **quality time** good, relaxing, peaceful time. You have all their attention. *I had some quality time with my parents.*
12. **recharge my batteries** to rest and relax, the same way a phone recharges. *Last weekend I recharged my batteries.*
13. **tentative plans** maybe, hopeful plans. *I have tentative plans to visit my grandparents.*

SPORTS & TALENTS

14. **killer abs, six pack** well-defined stomach muscles. *He's got killer abs.* • *My goal is to get a six pack.*
15. **last one picked** bad at sports, the last selected for teams. *I'm awful at sports. I was always the last one picked.*

TRAVEL

16. **at the last minute** suddenly. *At the last minute they had a vacancy. We decided at the last minute.*
17. **fall through** to fail, be canceled, ended. *Our plans fell through. Nobody was able to save enough money.*
18. **hassle** complicated. *Getting a visa to go to Nepal was a hassle.*
19. **jet lag** you're tired at odd times after a long flight. *I had jet lag for a week after I got back from Europe.*
20. **peak time, peak season** popular time, very crowded. *It's peak season. Let's stay home.*
21. **roughing it, rough it** hiking, camping, difficult. *My brother likes roughing it, especially camping.*
22. **travel light** to take very little luggage. *I travel light and wash clothes in the sink every night.*

He has a low tolerance for alcohol.

She's woozy. She's feeling woozy.

ELEVATOR SPEECH

How do you get, and relieve, stress? How's your social life?

I'm not much of a drinker but I enjoy party ***atmosphere****. My father says that alcohol is like everything else: "It can be good if you use it, bad if you abuse it." My first semester at university was party time. I drank a lot. You could say I was a* ***weekend warrior****: study during the week, and* ***party animal*** *on the weekends. My grades* ***suffered****. So, I became a* ***teetotaler****. That got real boring real quick. So, now I have a beer or two,* ***get a buzz,*** *and try to stay there. I'm not a* ***night owl****, so I'm usually home by midnight, with of course the* ***midnight munchies****. Eating after I get home tends to eliminate* ***hangovers****. Overall, I have kind of a split personality. On Saturday I'm* ***always on the go****, and on Sunday I'm a* ***couch potato.*** *Sleeping and watching TV all day long. In sum, heavy drinking was a phase that I went through.* ***Been there, done that****. Basically, I'm a* ***happy camper****. I rarely* ***get the blues****. And when I do, I just go jogging. After jogging for 10K, whatever problems I had disappeared. Mark Twain once said:* ***"80% of all the things I worried about never happened."*** 204 words

Social drinkers

Weekend warriors

Binge drinker

Toolbars

You can go to YouTube and watch many tutorials (in English)on PowerPoint and Keynote.

To get good at something, you do it many times. To do it many times, it helps if it's interesting. You do not need high tech skills to make a good presentation. However, playing with and learning tech can make the assignment interesting. And, better tech skills will help you get a better job.

1 HOME Send to Back and Bring to Front are very useful, for example, to move text from behind a photo, and vice versa.

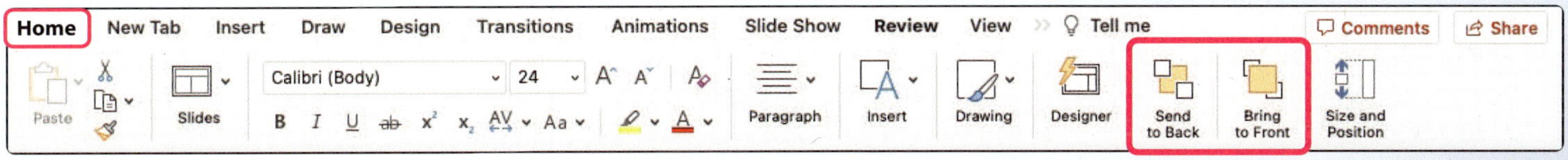

2 INSERT You can insert photos, charts, video and audio.

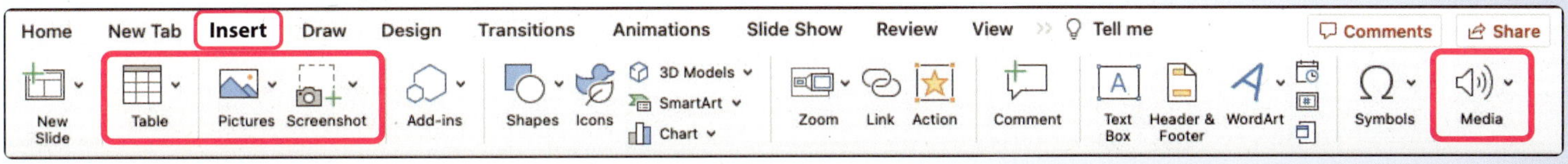

3 TRANSITIONS Many choices for slide transitions, how long the transitions take, and sound effects.

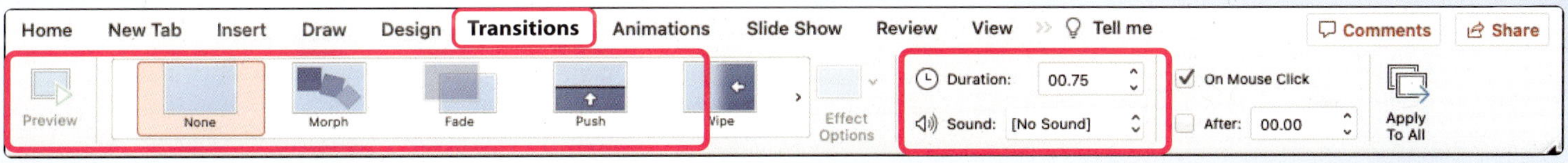

3 ANIMATIONS, and effect to emphasize

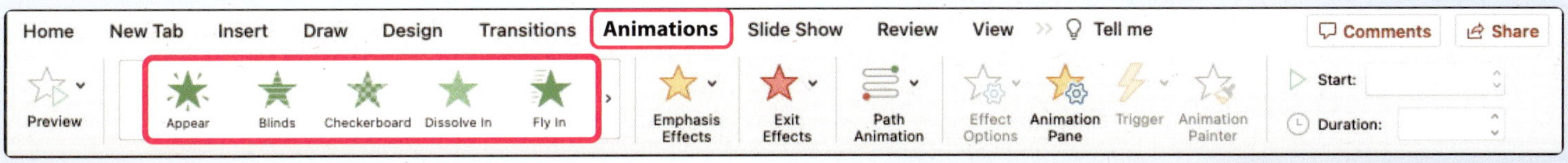

5 RECORD your presentation

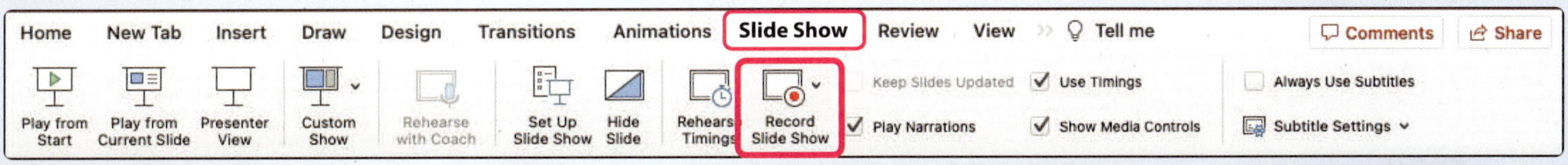

6 SPELL CHECK!

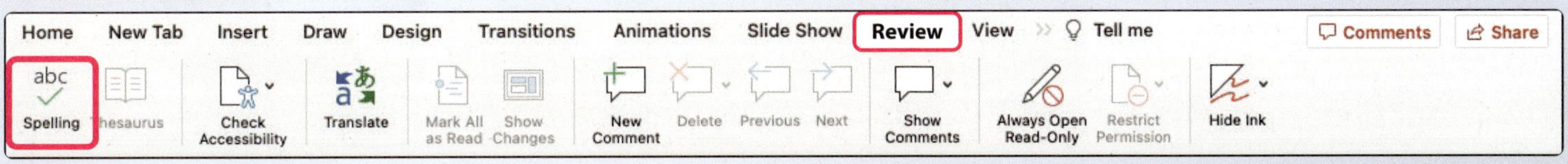

There's more info on page 110

ESSAY

This unit gives you the opportunity to talk about how you relax, your hobbies, interests, skills, travels, clubs.

If you answer the first few questions on a job interview clearly and confidently, they might ask you something like:
What do you like to do in your free time?

They want to see how well you can express yourself on an easy topic that you know well.

OUTLINE

INTRODUCTION

Half and half

1. Socially
2. Physically
3. Mentally

1 Socially

Always on the go
Social butterfly
Doer, not a viewer

2 Physically

Action addict
Extreme sports
Volunteer work

3 Mentally

Like to read
Watch documentaries
History books

CONCLUSION

1. Socially
2. Physically
3. Mentally

Are you an action addict or a couch potato?

I think they are right when they say that opposites attract. My father was in the paratroopers in the Army, he's an **action addict**. On the other hand, my mother's idea of a good time is reading a good book. Therefore, you could say I'm half and half. **Socially** and **physically** I'm **addicted to action**. I love **socializing** with people and I'm into **extreme sports**. However, **mentally** I'm like my mother. I relax by **kicking back** and reading and watching TV and YouTube.

Socially, I'm **always on the go.** You could call me a **social butterfly**, going from event to event. On the weekends I'm **always on the go**, never home. I really like outdoor activities, like live concerts and festivals. Two years ago I saw BTS live and it was awesome. So much energy on stage, and in the crowd. But, I'm also a doer, not just a viewer. Every year since I was about 10 I've participated in the Buddha parade in Seoul.

Physically also, I'm an **action addict**. I'm into fitness and I love **extreme sports**, such as **zipline, bungee jumping**, **scuba diving** and **white water rafting**. I got my scuba diving certificate last year. I like camping and **roughing it**, and every summer I do **volunteer work** in the countryside. I like the great outdoors, especially mountains. Whenever I'm on vacation I've just got to climb to the top of the highest peak in the area. My goal this year is to run the Seoul marathon.

Mentally for relaxing, I'm like my mom. I'm a people person, but I also enjoy my time alone. I like to read, mainly military history and biographies. I have about 20 Ebooks on my phone and iPad that I read when I'm on the subway. And on TV and Netflix there are plenty of military documentaries. On YouTube I can find a lot of lectures by the authors of books, such as Niall Ferguson, Andew Roberts and Max Hastings.

So there you have it. **Socially** and **physically**, I'm an **action addict**. I love being active with friends, and I love the great outdoors. But then there's the **Yin and Yang**. **Mentally,** I'm a **couch potato** like my mom. I love reading and watching, and I'll often go to **Wikipedia.com** to get background information. In sum, I **get a buzz** socially with friends, I get a **rush** from the great outdoors, and I **recharge my batteries** by reading and watching. 415 words

Always on the go

Action addict

History buff

Topics

1. What's more important to you, your major or your club?
2. What gives you stress: parents, professors, grades, friends, commuting, money, boy or girlfriend?
3. What are your top 3 sources of stress?
4. How do you relieve stress?
5. Are you a social butterfly or an action addict?
6. Are you a party animal or a party pooper?
7. On the weekends, do you rest, meet your friends, or study?
8. What's your favorite sport, or exercise, or weekend activity? Top 3?

INTRODUCTION

Hook ____________________

Topic Sentence ____________________

1 ________	2 ________	3 ________
a ________	a ________	a ________
b ________	b ________	b ________
c ________	c ________	c ________

CONCLUSION

Result / Implication ____________________

Getting stress from a professor

Happy loner, relieving stress (and saving money)

Advice

Your essay and presentation should be clear, cogent, cohesive and persuasive.
Most important, interesting.

WRITING ADVICE

1. **Don't try to write War and Peace.** Your Essay and Presentation follow a formula: Introduction, 123, Conclusion. It's your life, you know the information, insert that information into the template.
2. **Essays have transitions from paragraph to paragraph.** Presentations do not have transitions. The information is often in bullet points or numbers, 1, 2, 3, first, second, third.
3. **While writing your essay, your thinking improves.** Therefore, your conclusion is often better than your introduction. So, make your conclusion your introduction, and make another conclusion, perhaps with some of your introduction.
4. **As you copy and past from Word to PPT, you will notice mistakes.** Fix them, in your essay also. Even without input from your professor, your writing improves because you find so many of your own silly mistakes.
5. **Also, your thinking often improves,** and you find shorter, better ways of saying the same thing. Good.

PRESENTATION ADVICE

1. **ADD PASSION!** You are selling a product. The product is yourself.
2. **Don't waste your time.** Make a presentation that you can use later. Something that will improve your speaking, and vocabulary, in a topic that will help you get a job, or you will use very often in social situations.
3. **When you practice narrating, you will notice text and visual mistakes, fix them.** There will be mistakes in spelling and grammar.
4. **Consistency, check carefully for consistency.** Text size, boldness, italics, color, margins, spacing. Are the slide transitions consistent? Are they the same time duration? Are there too many different transition types?
5. **When you practice narrating, you will make bloopers and notice audio mistakes, fix them.**
6. **Add emphasis with your voice**. Put some feeling into it. Improve your pronunciation and articulation, and where you should speak slower, or faster.
7. **Sometimes**, you will think, '*This is important, it deserves a slide of its own.*' Other times, you will combine 2 minor slides into 1 major slide.
8. **After you fix all the mistakes in your Essay and Presentation, save it as a them as a template.** In this way, you don't have to spend a lot of time getting the next format correct. Just open your first templates and insert your new information and photos.
9. **If you have a friend in class, exchange videos with them.** Point out each others mistakes, and maybe make suggestions on how to make it better.
10. **Your first presentation will take the longest.** Everything you do is new. After that, every presentation is easier and takes less time. Use that extra time to work on your voice.

Your professor will have to watch many presentations.
Above all, make it interesting, and show your passion.

2ND CONVERSATION TEST 6

The instructions are simple: *Do it again.*

1st test

2nd test Always new partners

You can prove you improved

B20 Kim, Me-lee

This took me 90 minutes

	How many times I spoke	Average words per turn	Total words I spoke
Midterm test	46	8.6	400
Final test	54	15.5	480
	Improvement	80%	20%

Thus, my speaking improved 50% this semester.

VOCABULARY

ROMANCE	PART-TIME JOB	FREE TIME
love at first sight	workaholic	weekend warrior
high maintenance	cash poor	couch potato
ghost	flunky	spontaneous
pretty boy	materialistic	social butterfly
henpecked		

The top 5 mistakes and how to fix them.

1. No, I didn't heard about that.
   No, I didn't hear about that.
2. I have never been gone to there.
   I've never been there.
3. I am interesting in that.
   I am interested in that major.
4. What is your best favorite movie?
   What is your favorite movie?
5. Will you go to a festival or them park on this winter vacation?
   Will you go to any festivals or theme park this winter vacation?

---

1. Usually I'm weekend warriors, but last weekend I stayed at home because this week is midterm exam, so I was staying at home and studying for midterm exam. What did you do last weekend?
2. No, I didn't heard about that.
3. Last weekend I was couch potato. What about you?
4. I don't like gory films. I like superhero movies, like the Avengers and Ironman.

When you compare your first and second test data, you'll see your speaking improvement.

AVERAGE WORDS increased 80%

Longer speaking is smoother speaking.

TOTAL WORDS increased 20%

In the same amount of time, 20% more words.

This means shorter pauses and fewer pauses.

Does speaking really improve 50%?

ABSOLUTELY. All students have had grammar for 10 years, but most are beginning speakers.

For most students, saying two English sentences in a row is 100% improvement.

Professor! I've been speaking English for 10 years, and my speaking has never improved 50%.

That's because you rarely speak English.

Part 2

How to Make a Presentation From A to Z

Presentations are like Tennis

You learn the rules in 15 minutes. All improvement after that comes after a lot of practice.

For detailed information, there are many videos on YouTube.
Watch as many times as you like. First, without subtitles, then with.

First, Make a List 1

Let's say your assignment is on TECHNOLOGY IN YOUR LIFE.

SHORT VERSION

1 Make a list 2 Put in categories 3 Sort by number 4 Put in order of importance

LONG VERSION

1 Make a list **The first thing you do it make a list of all the tech terms you can think of.**
They will often come out of your brain in random order. No worry, just keep thinking and writing.
Make 1 long list. For example, below left is a list of 20. Put the list on Excel, and put them in alphabetical order.

2 Number and color code Go through the list and color code them by category.
For example, the Video apps in blue. After you have the categories colored, number the categories, for example:

1 Video apps **2 Music** **3 Social apps** **4 Education program**

3 Sort by number Excel will sort your terms by numbers. Bada-bing! You have 4 categories. Well done.

4 Pick your top 3 categories There are 4 categories, but you only need 3. So, pick your top 3 categories, put them in order of importance, then pick your three specific examples:

There's your outline. You're good to go. Add some specific examples: **why** you like them, **what** you use them for, **how** you use them, **how often** you use them, **how long** you watch them, and your **level of expertise**.

1 Make a list

1	Apple Music
2	Apple TV
3	Disney
4	Excel
5	Facebook
6	Illustrator
7	Instagram
8	Kakao Talk
9	Keynote
10	MS Word
11	Netflix
12	Pandora
13	Powerpoint
14	Shazam
15	Snapchat
16	Spotify
17	TikTok
18	Twitter
19	WhatsApp
20	YouTube

2 Color code & number

2	Apple Music
1	Apple TV
1	Disney
4	Excel
3	Facebook
4	Illustrator
3	Instagram
3	Kakao Talk
4	Keynote
4	MS Word
1	Netflix
2	Pandora
4	Powerpoint
2	Shazam
3	Snapchat
2	Spotify
1	TikTok
2	Twitter
3	WhatsApp
1	YouTube

3 Sort by number

1	Apple TV
1	Disney
1	Netflix
1	Tiktok
1	YouTube
2	Apple Music
2	Pandora
2	Shazam
2	Spotify
3	Facebook
3	Instagram
3	Kakao Talk
3	Snapchat
3	Twitter
3	WhatsApp
4	Excel
4	Illustrator
4	Keynote
4	MS Word
4	Powerpoint

4 Pick your top 3

1	**VIDEO**
	Netflix
	YouTube
	Tiktok
2	**SOCIAL APPS**
	Kakao
	Facebook
	Snapchat
3	**EDUCATION**
	Keynote
	iMovie
	Illustrator

Before Excel, you would brainstorm

In this century:

1. Make a list
2. Sort by number
3. Put in order of importance

THERE ARE 3 PARTS

Relax. Essays and Presentations are not some big mysterious thing. They're like a movie. They have a beginning, middle, and end.

Simple version:	Introduction, Body, Conclusion
Academic version:	Introduction with 123, 123 Paragraphs, Conclusion with 123
Movie version:	Boy meets girl, boy loses girl, boy gets girl

1. INTRODUCTION
- Background sentence or Hook
- Topic Sentence
- 1, 2, 3

2. 123 Paragraphs
- Reason
- Specific examples
- Names, dates, places, time, duration

3. CONCLUSION
- Concluding (topic) sentence
- 1, 2, 3
- Background sentence or Implications

Think of your introduction and conclusion as twins.

(The photo of the twins adds emphasis, don't you think? That's why you use photos in your presentation.)

The same information, put another way.

1 **Introduction** that has an interesting hook, a topic sentence, and your 1, 2, 3 summarized.

2 **Three paragraphs** your three reasons, (first, second, third), with specific examples that prove your point.

3 **Conclusion** that repeats your topic sentence, and summarizes your 1, 2, 3.

Put another way

PREVIEW
This is what I'm going to say.
My parent are strict.
Here's how to make a hat.

DETAILS
Here's the details.
Here's proof they are strict.
Here's the steps to make a hat.

REVIEW
This is what I said.
My parents are so strict.
That's how to make a hat.

Preview, Do, Review

PREVIEW

HOOK The first sentence is usually the 'hook'. Something that hooks you, like a fish. It grabs you, gets your attention. It should be interesting and make you want to continue reading. Last weekend changed my life! OK, I would keep reading. I would expect to read details of how your life changed.

BACKGROUND SENTENCE The first sentence might also be called 'background knowledge'. It states why the topic is important. For example, if you're writing that your iPhone is your most important tech device, you might begin with Handheld technology has changed the world.

TOPIC SENTENCE Therefore, your first sentence is not necessarily your topic sentence. The topic sentence tells you what the essay is about. My iPhone is my most important tech device, because of 1, 2, 3.

1, 2, 3 First, second, third are your specific examples. I use it first for communication, second for entertainment, and third for education.

1, 2, 3 PARAGRAPHS

First, *I use it for **communication**. For example: Kakao, Facebook . . .*

Second, *I use it for **entertainment**. For example: YouTube, Netflix . . .*

Third, *I use it for **education**: Wikipedia, BBC, Watch videos on how to make a presentation.*

Each paragraphs gives SPECIFIC EXAMPLES why your iPhone is important. It's your life, you know the details.

REVIEW

The conclusion is a mirror of the introduction. You summarize or say the same thing (in the same order 1, 2, 3) in different words. You might also go for a boffo ending (like a hook) and include an implication (possible effect) regarding the future: Therefore, when the new iPhones come out, I'll be first in line.

MIRROR IMAGES

OFTEN, by the time you finish writing your introduction and 1, 2, 3, your thinking and writing has improved, and your conclusion is pretty darn good. In fact, it's better than your introduction!

So, switch them. Make your conclusion your introduction.

Then, write another conclusion (possibly using some of the introduction).

Professor. Wouldn't that be, well, repetitious?

Absolutely. To let someone know that something is important (like your birthday is next week), you keep repeating.

Why repeat so much?

Because, after the average person gets to a train station, they check their ticket 6 times before they sit down. SIX TIMES! People forget.

More repetition = more retention.

3 Types Of Format

1. You can download the MS Word template from the website. Delete the example information, and put your own.
2. Don't try to invent a new format.
   Don't try to write Harry Potter.
   Insert your information in the template.
3. You may make modifications to the template. If so, save YOUR template, and use that next time.
4. This is a speaking class. The writing makes your speaking more organized, which makes you appear more intelligent.
5. Your Essay is the organization, and script, of your Presentation.
6. For grading purposes, your essay is in a beauty contest. It will be graded only by appearance.

5-Paragraph Persuasive TOEFL Essay

I'm an extrovert, and here's why.

Engaging, background sentence x xxxxxxx xxxx xxx xxx xxxxxxxx xxxxx xxx. Xxxxxx xxxxxxxxxx xxxxx xxx. **I'm an extrovert. First**, xxxx xx xxxxx x, **second**, xxxx xxxxxx xxx **third**, xxxx xxxxxx. **Hook.** Xxxxxx xxxx xx xxxxx x xxxxxxx xxxx xxx xxxxxxxx xxxxx xxx.

First, xxxx xx xxxxx x xxxxxxx xxxx xxx xxx xxxxxxxx xxxxx xxx. Xxxxxx xxxx xx xxxxx x xxxxxxx xxxx xxx xxx xxxxx xxx. Xxxxx xxx. Xxxxxx xxxx xx xxxxx x xxxxxxx xxxx xxx xxx xxxxxxxx xxxxx xxx. Xxxxxx xxxx xx xxxxx x xxxxxxx xxxx xxx xxx xxxxxxxx xxxxx xxx.

Second, xxxx xx xxxxx x xxxxxxx xxxx xxx xxx xxxxxxxx xxxxx xxx. Xxxxxx xxxx xx xxxxx x xxxxxxx xxxx xxx xxx xxxxx xxx. Xxxxx xxx. Xxxxxx xxxx xx xxxxx x xxxxxxx xxxx xxx xxx xxxxxxxx xxxxx xxx. Xxxxxx xxxx xx x xxxxxxx xxxx xxx xxx xxxxxxxx xxxxx xxx.

Third xxxx xx xxxxx x xxxxxxx xxxx xxx xxx xxxxxxxx xxxxx xxx. Xxxxxx xxxx xx xxxxx x xxxxxxx xxxx xxx xxx xxxxx xxx. Xxxxx xxx. Xxxxxx xxxx xx xxxxx x xxxxxxx xxxx xxx xxx xxxxxxxx xxxxx xxx. Xxxxxx xxxx xx xxxxx x xxxxxxx xxxx xxx xxx xxxxxxxx xxxxx xxx.

In conclusion, xxxxxxx xxxx xxx xxx xxxxxxxx xxxxx xxx. Xxxxxx xxxx xxx xxxxxxxx xxxxx xxx. **I'm an extrovert. First**, xxxx xx xxxxx x ,**second**, xxxx xxx xxx **third**., xxx xxxxxx xxxxx xxx xx. **Hook.** Xxxxxx xxxx xx xxxxx xxxx xxx xxx xxxxxxxx xxxxx xxx.

350 Words

Good news, bad news • Yin & Yang

Modern Technology can be used, and abused.

Engaging, background sentence x xxxxxxx xxxx xxx xxx xxxxxxxx xxxxx xxx. Xxxxxx xxxxxxxxxx xxxxx xxx. **The good news is** xxxx xx xxxxx x xx. **The bad news is** xxxx xx xxxxx x xx. Xxxxxx xxxx xx xxxxx x xxxxxxx xxxx xxx xxx xxxxx xxx. Xxxxx xxx.

The good news, xxxx xx xxxxx x xxxxxxx xxxx xxx xxx xxxxxxxx xxxxx xxx. Xxxxxx xxxx xx xxxxx x xxxxxxx xxxx xxx xxx xxxxx xxx. Xxxxx xxx. Xxxxxx xxxx xx xxxxx x xxxxxxx xxxx xxx xxx xxxxxxxx xxxxx xxxxx x xxxx xx xxxxx x xxxxxxxxxx.

xxx xx xxxxx x xxxxxxx xxxx xxx xxx xxxxxxxx xxxxx xxx. Xxxxxx xxxx xx xxxxx x xxxxxxx xxxx xxx xxx xxxxx xxx. Xxxxx xxx. Xxxxxx xxxx xx xxxxx x xxxxxxx xxxx xxx xxx xxxxxxxx xxxxx xxx. Xxxxxx xxxx xx x xxxxxxx xxxx xxx xxx xxxxxxxx xxxxx xxx.

The bad news, xxxx xx xxxxx x xxxxxxx xxxx xxx xxx xxxxxxxx xxxxx xxx. Xxxxxx xxxx xx xxxxx x xxxxxxx xxxx xxx xxx xxxxx xxx. Xxxxx xxx. Xxxxxx xxxx xx xxxxx x xxxxxxx xxxx xxx xxx xxxxxxxx xxxxx xxxxx x xxxx xx xxxxx x xxxxxxx xxx.

xxx xx xxxxx x xxxxxxx xxxx xxx xxx xxxxxxxx xxxxx xxx. Xxxxxx xxxx xx xxxxx x xxxxxxx xxxx xxx xxx xxxxx xxx. Xxxxx xxx. Xxxxxx xxxx xx xxxxx x xxxxxxx xxxx xxx xxx xxxxxxxx xxxxx xxx. Xxxxxx xxxx xx x xxxxxxx xxxx xxx x'xx xxxxxxxx xxxxx xxx.

In conclusion, that's how technology can help people, and harm people. xxxxxxx xxxx xxx xxx xxxxxxxx xxxxx xxx. Xxxxxx xxxx xxx xxxxxxxx xxxxx xxx. xx xx xxxxx x xx. Xxxxxx xxxx xx xxxxx x xxxxxxx xxxx xxx xxx xxxxx xxx. Xxxxx xxx.

Information • Instruction

My courses this semester.

Background sentence x xxxxxxx xxxx xxx xxx xxxxxxxx xxxxx xxx. Xxxxxx xxxxxxxxxx xxxxx xxx. **I'm taking 6 courses.** xxxxxxx xxxx xxx xxx xxxxxxxx xxxxx xxx.

Math, xxxx xx xxxxx x xxxxxxx xxxx xxx xxx xxxxxxxx xxxxx xxx. Xxxxxx xxxx xx xxxxx x xxxxxxx xxxx xxx xxx xxxxx xxx. Xxxxx xxx. Xxxxxx xxxx xx xxxxx x xxxxxxx xxxx xxx xxx xxxxx xxx.

Ethics, xxxx xx xxxxx x xxxxxxx xxxx xxx xxx xxxxxxxx xxxxx xxx. Xxxxxx xxxx xx xxxxx x xxxxxxx xxxx xxx xxx xxxxx xxx. Xxxxx xxx. Xxxxxx xxxx xx xxxxx x xxxxxxx xxxx xxx xxx xxxxx xxx.

Computer, xxxx xx xxxxx x xxxxxxx xxxx xxx xxx xxxxxxxx xxxxx xxx. Xxxxxx xxxx xx xxxxx x xxxxxxx xxxx xxx xxx xxxxx xxx. Xxxxx xxx. Xxxxxx xxxx xx xxxxx x xxxxxxx xxxx xxx xxx

Science, xxxx xx xxxxx x xxxxxxx xxxx xxx xxx xxxxxxxx xxxxx xxx. Xxxxxx xxxx xx xxxxx x xxxxxxx xxxx xxx xxx xxxxx xxx. Xxxxx xxx. Xxxxxx xxxx xx xxxxx x xxxxxxx xx xxx xxxxx xxx.

History, xxxx xx xxxxx x xxxxxxx xxxx xxx xxx xxxxxxxx xxxxx xxx. Xxxxxx xxxx xx xxxxx x xxxxxxx xxxx xxx xxx xxxxx xxx. Xxxxx xxx. Xxxxxx xxx xxxxx x xxxxxxx xxxx xxx xxx xxxxx xxx.

Geography, xxxx xx xxxxx x xxxxxxx xxxx xxx xxx xxxxxxxx xxxxx xxx. Xxxxxx xxxx xx xxxxx x xxxxxxx xxxx xxx xxx xxxxx xxx. Xxxxx xxx. Xxxxxx xxxx xx xxxxx x xxxxxxx xxxx xxx xxx xxxxx xxx.

In conclusion, all my courses are hard. Xxxxxxxxxxxx xxxxx xxx. Xxxxxx xxxx xxx xxxxxxxx xxxxx xxxxxxxx xx Xxxxxxxxxxxx xxxxx xxx. Xxxxxx xxxx xxx xxxxxxxx

Look at the two essays below. Imagine they are on your university entrance exam. You are told to read the essay and answer: **Is the idea good or bad? Why? Give specific details.** You have 3 minutes.

The instructions state that both essays contain the same information. You can read either 1 or 2.

Which do you choose?

1

Is this a good idea? Why or why not?

Ni voluptam idebisciam nim sit volor autem fugiatias dessusam volorestem eatiost, qui doluptio mincturestio inctiatia conecero quibust, odia voloribea dolenditas sim voluptatemEcto tectium vel moloritat perumet urempor restisi milibus min nonet es quam doluptatem cores res comnis et occaborio te net pra nime mo volor moloruntus eaquatio. Pudipsum id moluptatent ligniet aut quibeaqui re comnis aditis rest acimint ius nonse eati cus eveles nosam eatem ex et exceptatatus atibus, sinvendae rese quodit utem comnita dis assed quiaerati dolorem. Cest, officabo. Et aut volupta quia quam dolore quam volo es de simodis magnatur?Hendest, quo dolupti rectis susae. Adigend ignatis peliaeres audiam quia volupici dusdam qui odio. Ritaspe nobis voluptat quosti odis il et harum velecae optias iuscien tiorporit et dolut a consequ unturibusdae reriae volorum, volut alibust, te voloriam eruption ni dolorae suntempor aut quis ate dolenis et ut officiet modis ma verumetus dit essimus erchicia iusdam quaturi soluptaque everition eum in earuptate pereste elic tempell uptur? Qui odis pa nullique voluptatam hit voloruntiis reriosapicae poressit aut qui occum rempe num volupta temosa vellistia soluptis dolorum quas sumqui offictet ut et aut aut quo que voluptaqui bea comnihicium que mil et utemporro mincili busdam et por arciduciis autatur, ium is mi, cum que ent qeritiae. Natur a simpore praectem volorib erspelliquam ipienda nectatatem volupti blantestiis aborepe rcitibu stiatibus autat ari ut ped eaqui bea iditatis aut lacea volor sedist odissimus molupit unti quia consequi sitat. Ritaspe nobis voluptat quosti odis il et harum velecae optias iuscien tiorporit et dolut a consequ unturibusdae reriae volorum, volut alibust, te voloriam eruption ni dolorae suntempor aut quis ate dolenis et ut officiet modis ma verumetus dit essimus erchicia iusdam.

2

Is this a good idea? Why or why not?

Ni voluptam idebisciam nim sit volor autem fugiatias dessusam volorestem eatiost, qui doluptio mincturestio inctiatia conecero quibust, odia voloribea dolenditas sim voluptatemEcto tectium vel moloritat perumet urempor restisi milibus min nonet es quam doluptatem cores res comnis et occaborio te net pra nime mo volor moloruntus eaquatio.

First, id moluptatent ligniet aut quibeaqui re comnis aditis rest acimint ius nonse eati cus eveles nosam eatem ex et exceptatatus atibus, sinvendae rese quodit utem comnita dis assed quiaerati dolorem. Cest, officabo. Et aut volupta quia quam dolore quam volo es de simodis magnatur? Qui odis pa nullique voluptatam.

Second, quo dolupti rectis susae. Adigend ignatis peliaeres audiam quia volupici dusdam qui odio. Ritaspe nobis voluptat quosti odis il et harum velecae optias iuscien tiorporit et dolut a consequ unturibusdae reriae volorum, e suntempor aut quis ate dolenis et ut officiet modis ma verumetus dit essimus. Ritaspe nobis voluptat quosti odis il et harum.

Third, odis pa nullique voluptatam hit voloruntiis reriosapicae poressit aut qui occum rempe num volupta temosa vellistia soluptis dolorum quas sumqui offictet ut et aut aut quo que voluptaqui bea comnihicium que mil et utemporro mincili busdam et por arciduciis autatur, ium is mi, cum que ent quam ex es et et apel eles eat omniene nos eicipsa erferfe ribus.

In conclusion, Ritaspe nobis voluptat quosti odis il et harum velecae optias iuscien tiorporit et dolut a consequ unturibusdae reriae volorum, volut alibust, te voloriam eruption ni dolorae suntempor aut quis ate dolenis et ut officiet modis ma verumetus dit essimus erchicia iusdam. Qui odis pa nullique voluptatam hit voloruntiis reriosapicae poressit aut.

Wow. That's a lot of words!

I have to carefully read **THE WHOLE THING**.. There's no pattern, no emphasis, just a whole bunch of words.

I have to read **every single word** to figure out if it's good or bad. Then, I have to read it again, to find the reasons. And then I have to find the specific details. *Professor! English is not my first language!*

This looks organized.

The conclusion will tell me if it's good or bad, and the 3 paragraphs will give the 3 specific reasons why.

Bada-bing.

Whenever you have an academic reading, read the conclusion first. Then the introduction. Repeat until you understand the thesis. They will both have the same thesis idea, for example: ***Drugs are bad.***

AFTER you understand that the paper is about drugs are bad, then you look in the rest of the paper for ***why*** they are bad. **REPEAT**. Do not look for details of the main idea, until you know what the main idea is.

Why read the conclusion first? Because in the introduction writers try to make it interesting, so that you will keep reading. The conclusion is where the writer has ***one last chance*** to make you understand. So they are brief, and clear.

The correct format will quickly show your professor – or boss – that you are capable of academic work.

HOW TO BEGIN & END

Try to start your presentation
like a *Mission Impossible* movie. ACTION!

Imagine one of the photos below is the first slide of your presentation, and you say:

I'm an action addict, and I can prove it.

I'm a joiner, and I can prove it.

If that was the first slide of your presentation, your classmates would surely keep watching!

START A PRESENTATION

1. **You can introduce yourself, but everybody already knows who you are.**
   (And think of your poor professor: they have to watch 20 presentations that begin with, *Hi, I'm a student at...*
2. **Tell a story.** *When my mother was in college, female doctors were very rare.*
3. **Open with a hook, rhetorical question, interesting questions, statistic, chart, interesting fact.**
   Did you know that half of all university students are below average? But not me!
   Your presentation then proves how you are above average.
4. **Ask a 'what if' question.** *What if I got my dream job? Would I actually be able to do it?*
   Your presentation then proves how qualified and skilled you are.
5. **Use a powerful quote.** Mark Twain said *"Eighty percent of all the things I worried about never happened." Therefore, I'm not going to worry about getting a job. I'm going to party at college.*
6. **You might do a quick search and come up with an interesting statistic.** For example, if your topic is technology: *Did you know that the average Korean teenager spends 2 hours a day on their phone?*
7. **For dramatic effect,** you can use **BIG BOLD TEXT**. And special effects with the text, zoom it in, or out.
   You can raise your voice ***DRAMATICALLY!*** Let them know that this will be a very interesting presentation!

Your first slide and introduction set the tone for your presentation.

Murder mysteries begin with a certain kind of music. Romantic comedies begin with another kind of music. In the same way, your introduction sets the tone for your presentation. If you start off with a quiet monotone voice saying, *Hi. It's nice to meet you, I'm . . . blah blah blah*, well, that's not good.

Below is the introduction to a short essay. The first sentence is the hook. The second sentence is the topic sentence, and the third sentence is the 1, 2, 3.

> *I am such a wonderful, smart, nice, and kind daughter. However, my parents are very strict. They are pretty much strict about everything, but mainly they are strict about my grades, my allowance and my curfew.*

After reading that introduction, you expect that you will read about specific **grades** (ABC) specific **money** ($50 a week) and specific **times** (midnight). You'll be able to follow. You won't be thinking, *What the heck is she talking about? Where is she going with this?*

You'll be able to follow along and retain more. When she repeats something 2 or 3 times, you will know that's important.

END A PRESENTATION

1. **Your conclusion should be the twin of your introduction.**
   That's why you should hire me: my superior education, experience and ability.
2. **Use a powerful quote:** *Therefore, my motto for college is carpe beerum.* (Seize the beer.)
3. **State the implications.** *Being an intern will give me the skills, experience, and connections to get my dream job.*
4. **Have a plot twist. A surprise ending can make an average presentation a great presentation!**
   (For example, the Korean movie ***Oldboy*** had a great plot twist.)

This could be your last slide.
Or, it could be your second-to-last slide.

I'm an action addict, and here was my proof.

And this would be your last slide.

My next adventure will be scuba diving

TIP: Have fun.
If you have fun making the presentation, it will an interesting presentation.

EXAMPLES & EVIDENCE

I'm an outdoor person and I love to travel. ***Prove it.***

OK. Here's a photo of my boyfriend and me on a road trip along the Pacific Coast Highway, from San Francisco to Los Angeles. This was in the summer of 2016, and it took two weeks.

Where, when, who, how, how long, how far?

The highway, cities, dates, and duration are SPECIFIC details, that help prove your point.

That big photo is nice for your first slide, but do you have 3 more specific examples?

Jogging on Waikiki Beach in Hawaii

Canoeing in Sarlat, France

Roughing it in Colombia

Photos with your face are very convincing. If you don't have photos, that's OK. Do what you can. You can go to Google Image and screen capture. Photos are evidence, and they make your presentation more interesting, entertaining and convincing.

When you give details about those photos and experiences, you text will easily be long enough for a 5-minute presentation. Then, **add emphasis** to show which place was the **MOST** fun, interesting, friendly, memorable experience. Any why.

Have you ever traveled abroad? is a common job interview question. A presentation like this would be great preparation.

If you love to travel but haven't travelled much, your presentation could tell where you would like to go, and why.

PHOTOS

My girlfriend has high self-esteem

Global Warming is harmful to extroverted polar bears

BODY LANGUAGE

TEXT

Say it	This is important.
Bigger, bold, capitalize	**This is IMPORTANT!**
Make it red	**This is IMPORTANT!**
Center it	**THIS IS IMPORTANT**

INFOGRAPHICS

1. **To show and emphasize information**, **Excel**, **PowerPoint** and **Keynote** have many types of charts and graphs.
2. Enter your data on **Excel**, and click on the type of chart you want.
3. In **PowerPoint** and **Keynote** your charts can be animated.

Use data to emphasize your point

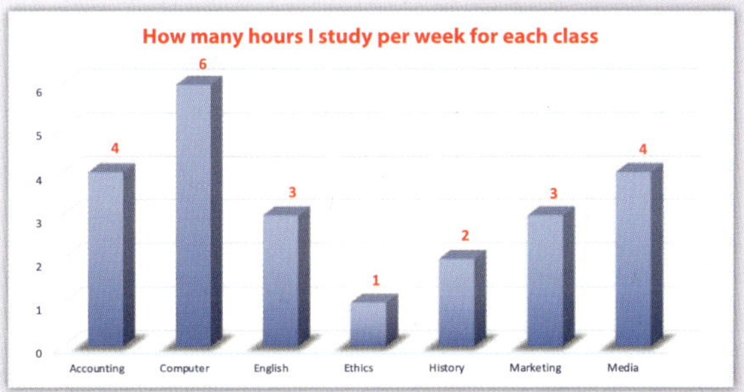

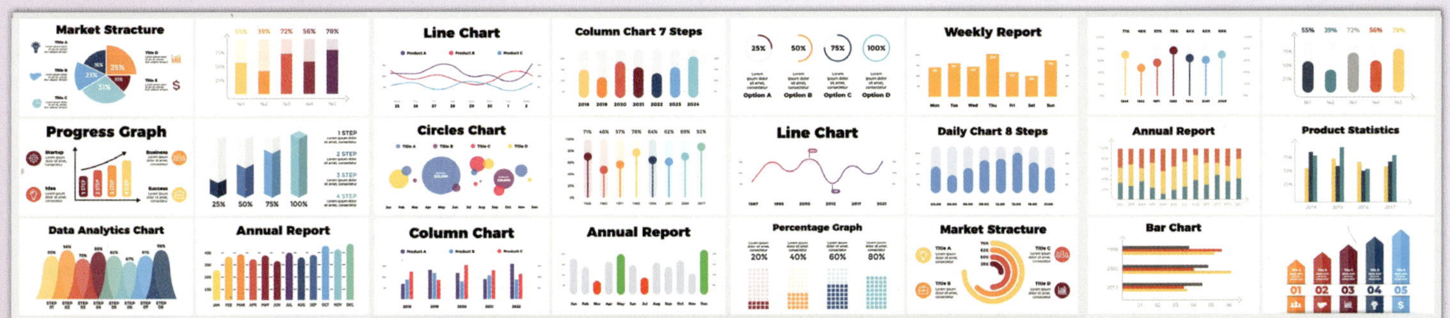

NARRATED VIDEO

Presentations are like playing tennis.

Everybody knows the rules. To get better you do it many times.

Record

Watch and make notes

Do it again

Repeat many times

Every time you watch you will notice presentation mistakes. Fix them.

Every time you record, you will make bloopers (speaking mistakes). Fix them.

After doing this 10 times, your presentation, and voice, will be much improved.

BEFORE RECORDING

1. **Consistency check**. Before recording, go through every slide and look for consistency mistakes. Font size, color, bold, italic. Text is consistently centered, flush left, flush right. Background colors, margins, slide transitions uniform.
2. **Voice check**. Practice recording your voice at different distances from the microphone, for example 15, 30 and 45cm. Determine which distance is best, and use that.
3. **Length check.** Record and narrate your presentation to see if it's about the correct length.

RECORDING **As you record, you will make mistakes. You have 2 basic choices.**

START OVER Perhaps many times.
KEEP GOING and edit out the mistakes on a video program.

If you start over many times, it may take an hour to make a 3-minute, mistake-free video. On the other hand, you could edit out many mistakes in about 30 minutes.

1. For your practice recordings, you can save in low quality video. This saves memory and time.
2. When all is perfect, save your video at high quality settings.

SAVE & UPLOAD

1. **Save your presentation as a TEMPLATE.** And for your next presentation all your slides, colors, text and transitions will be correct and consistent. Your next presentation will take half the time.
2. When all is good, UPLOAD.

No memorizing. Much practice.

Find an empty classroom

Record yourself presenting in classroom. Live! on video.

Record in class while your partners watch, and ask questions

In an empty classroom, you can

A) Bring your presentation on a USB and use the classroom computer to project your presentation onto the big board.

B) Put your laptop on the desk, and place it so that you can see your presentation.

---

1. In both cases, you can secretly see your notes, and advance the slides with a wireless clicker.
2. Record with you phone. You might put it far way in the middle of the classroom, so that you (at the podium) and the whole big board can be seen. You might get a friend to video you.
3. If you are a group, one of your partners can video. For extra realism, your partners could ask questions.
4. If you are in a small group, you could take turns videoing, and giving feedback to, each other.

Whether you narrate or self record, you can edit the video.

EDIT iMovie tools that can enhance your audio.

1 AUDIO raise or lower the sound

2 EQUALIZER You can **Reduce background noise,** and use the **Voice Enhance** setting

3 SPEED If your video is a just a little bit long, for example, 3:05 minutes, you can adjust the speed so that it's 3:00. This can make the sound sharper and your pronunciation more crisp.

iMovie tools 1 2 3

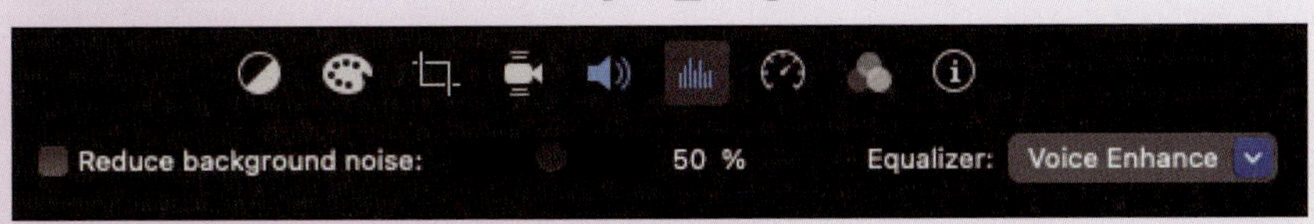

IN PERSON

Reading out loud in class will not impress anyone

Everybody learned to read in the first grade. It's not an academic skill.

Well-educated people speaking clearly, confidently, and articulately.

That's the purpose of your presentation.

NO READING!

APPEARANCE (Looks are important)

Wash your hair, dress nice, stand up straight.

1. If you look professional, and it appears that your presentation is important to you, your audience will think it's important, and pay attention.
2. If you look casual and informal, then your audience will think it's not important, and will not pay attention.
3. No hats! Your eyes are an important communicative tool.
4. If your presentation is great, you can use it in your job application package. However, if your clothes are too casual, you'll have to do the presentation again with better clothes.

STAND UP STRAIGHT

You represent your parents and grandparents. Stand up straight like an important, high self-esteem, educated person.

INVISIBLE NOTES

If you are presenting using a class computer, which is in a podium, here are some variations for using notes:

1. At the bottom of each slide you can have some notes. These note are only visible to you, the audience cannot see them.
2. If you are presenting using your Notebook, place it on a desk at the front, facing you, so that only you can see the computer screen.
3. Thus, instead of holding notes in your hand, you read notes from the computer or notebook monitor.

From her notebook, she can see her notes, which slide is next, and how much time she has left.

Stand to the side, use the clicker to advance the slides, and maintain eye contact.

Presenting in the 21st century requires speaking ability, and technical ability.
Sometimes, solving technical problems before presenting is harder than presenting. Be prepared.

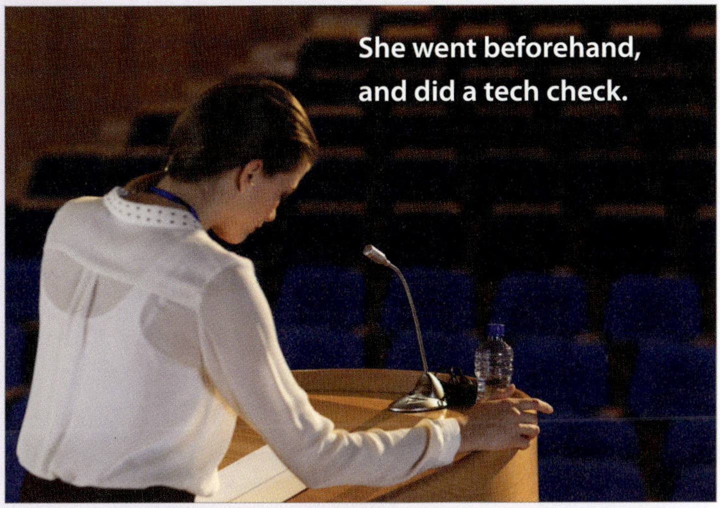

Go to the classroom before class, or days before class, and do a tech check. You may also a try an empty class that has similar equipment. **You do not want to have tech problems in front of the whole class.**

TYPICAL CLASS SCENARIO

You're presenting in a class that has a computer and podium with an overhead projector.

1. You can use that, or use your laptop, and connect that to class computer. An advantage of using your laptop is that you can place it on a table in between you and the audience, and use it as a teleprompter.
2. Another advantage of using your laptop is that you are certain that your presentation will format and look correctly. Sometimes, the class computer may not contain the text you used in your presentation, and sometimes the class computer will not play certain types of video that may be embedded in your presentation.
3. You can use your phone to record yourself. Set it up on the back of the class, and adjust the zoom. A classmate can video, and you video them. If your presentation is good, and you are well-dressed, you can use the video when look for a job.

WALK AROUND

Be an animated action figure! For most of your presentation you may stay behind the podium, but when you want to emphasize something, you make walk around and point at the screen (and of course use your voice for emphasis).

WARNING, if your phone is too close to you, when you walk around you'll go out of the picture. So, go there early and find a good place in the rear to put your camera on a tripod.

ABOUT READING NOTES

Nobody wants to look at the top of your head while you read notes. You learned how to read in the first grade. You will not impress anyone by reading out loud. Reading is in front of people not an academic or business skill.

Slide & Text Animation

There are many ways to introduce your information. Below are some options.

TEXT can appear:

All at once

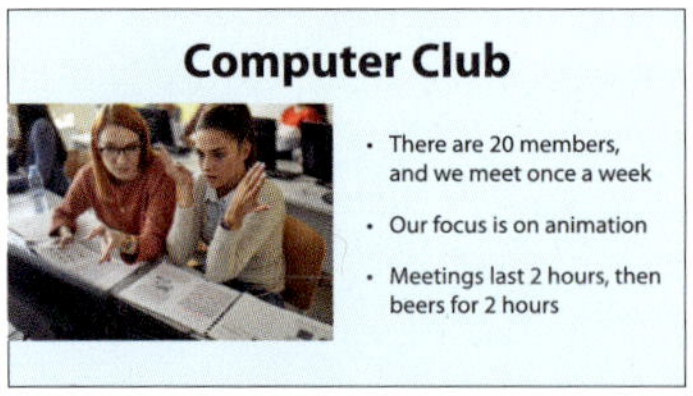

Line by line

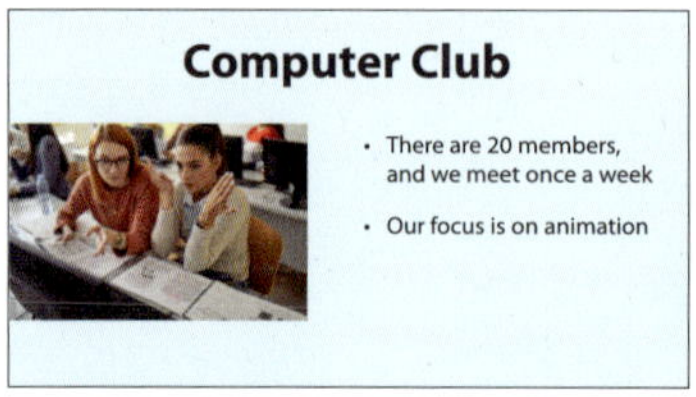

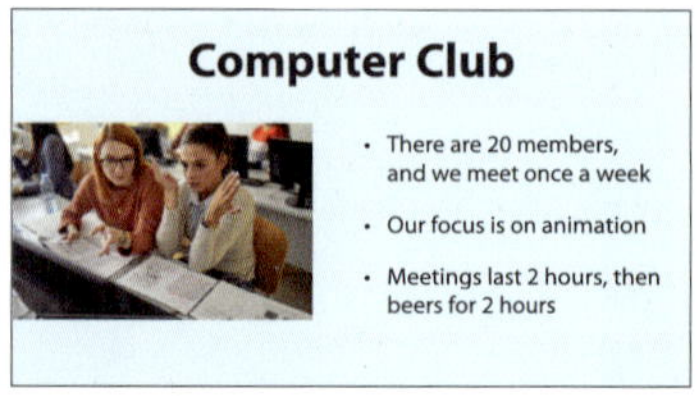

PHOTOS can appear big, one on each slide

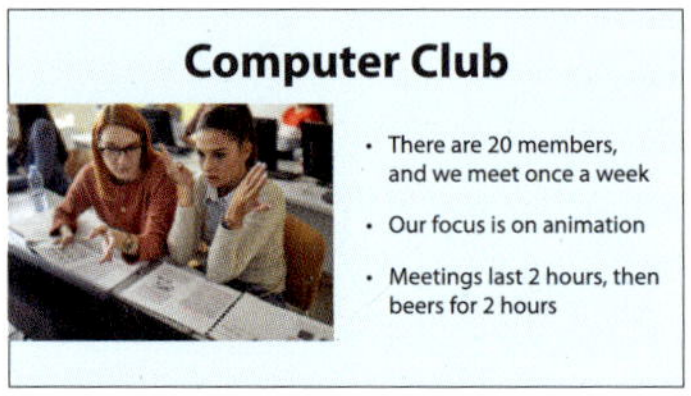

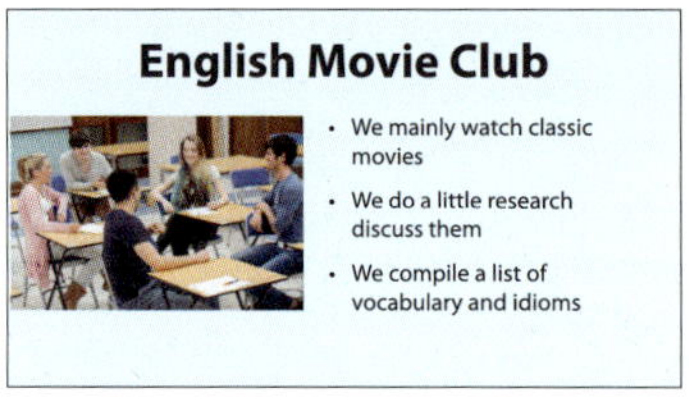

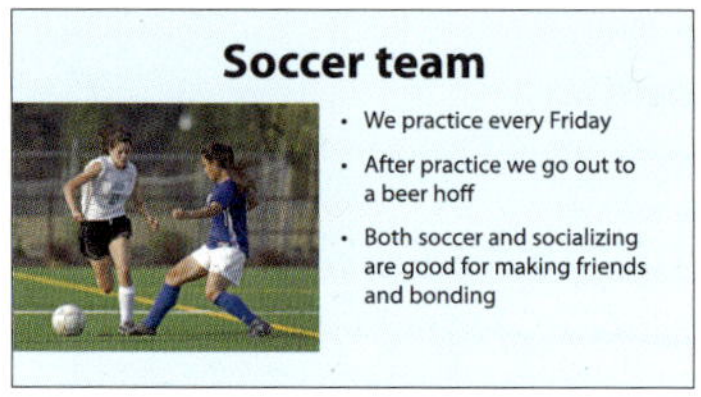

or, a small photo magically appears every slide, with all 3 photos on the last slide.

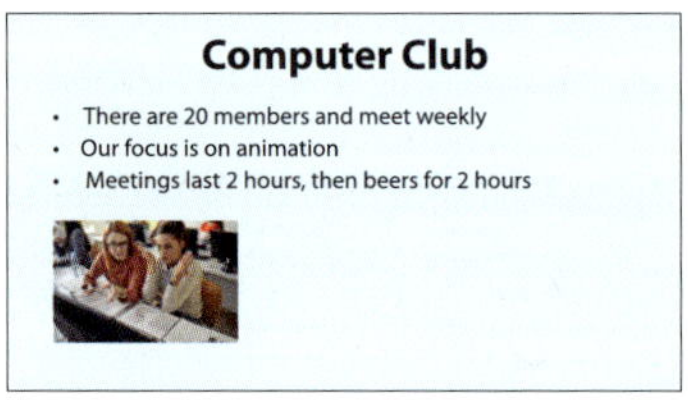

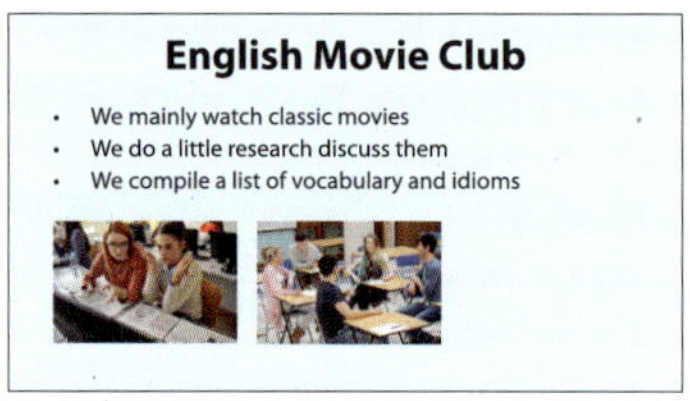

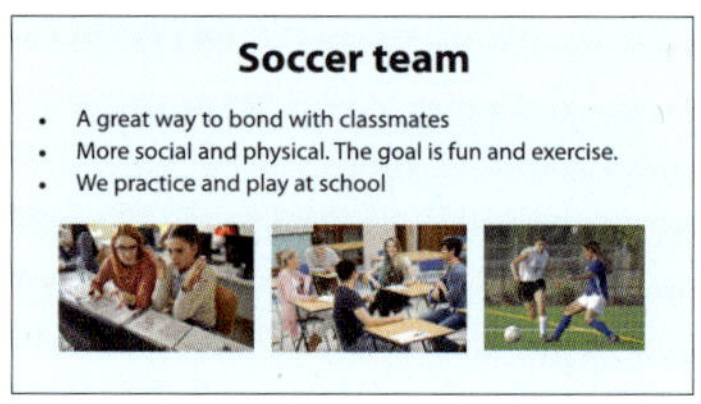

TRANSITIONS

1. Transitions after the **Introduction** and before the **Conclusion**, could be strong, such a "door opening" for 2 seconds.
2. The slide transitions for the headers, (1, 2, 3) could be emphasized, such as "page turning" for 1.5 seconds.
3. For the rest of the slides, there might be no transitions, with the transition time of .4 or .5 seconds.
4. The **changes from section to section** should be clear and emphatic. It lets you know something new is starting.
5. The **changes within sections** should be subtle, showing that it's a continuation.
6. **For dramatic effect** (and entertainment) you can add sound effects (such as applause) after some slides or sections.

Transition Toolbar

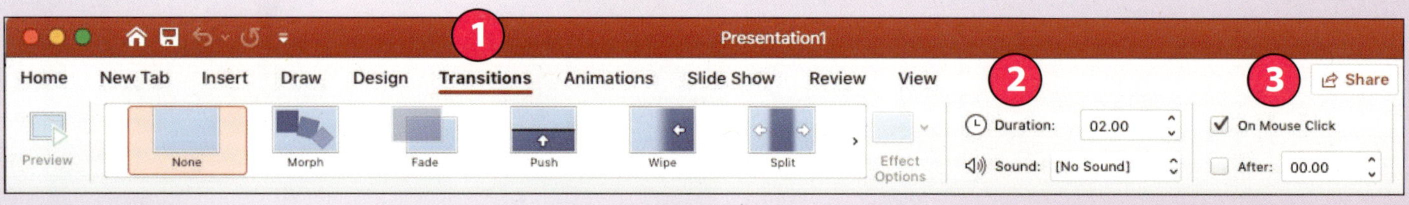

1. **TRANSITIONS:** from slide to slide.
2. **DURATION:** How long it takes before the next slide.
3. **ON MOUSE CLICK:** The next slide begins automatically, after .5 seconds, or when you click the mouse.

Here's a basic, starter plan:

1. After your introduction, use a **PAGE CURL** or **CUBE** to signal that the introduction is over. (Duration of about 1.5 seconds)
2. The transition time for slide-to-slide within in the first section, can be .4 or .5 seconds. No special effects, just subtle.
3. To signal that the first section is over, use the same PAGE CURL or CUBE. This indicates that section 1 is over, and a new section will begin.
4. After the last slide of section 3, you might use PAGE CURL or CUBE, or a more dramatic transition, to signal that the dramatic conclusion is about to begin.
5. In short: Transitions within a section are subtle. To signal that the content is similar.
   Transitions from section to section are animated, to signal the section is ending, and a new one is beginning.

Slide Transition Choices

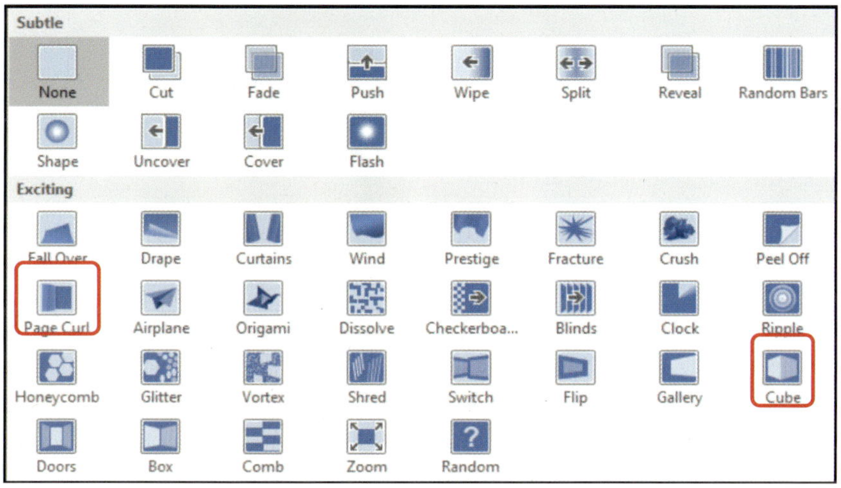

Text Animation Choices

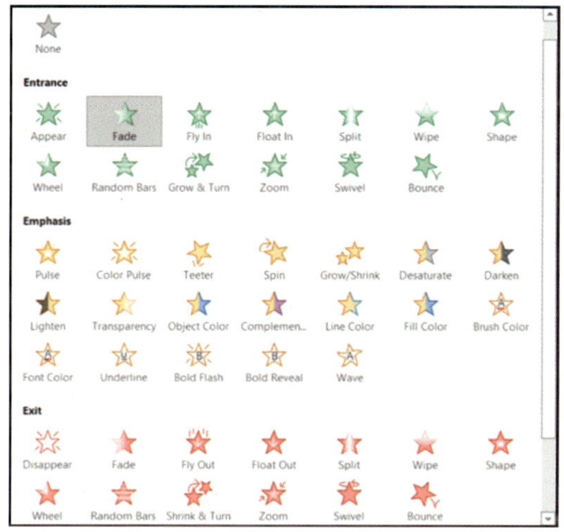

In Powerpoint you can see details of each slide, and your whole presentation at once.

You can type **notes** at the bottom to help when presenting.

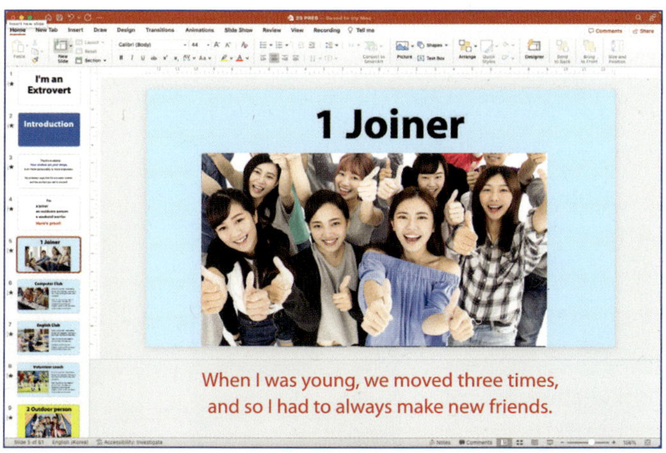

You can check that fonts, color, margins are consistent.

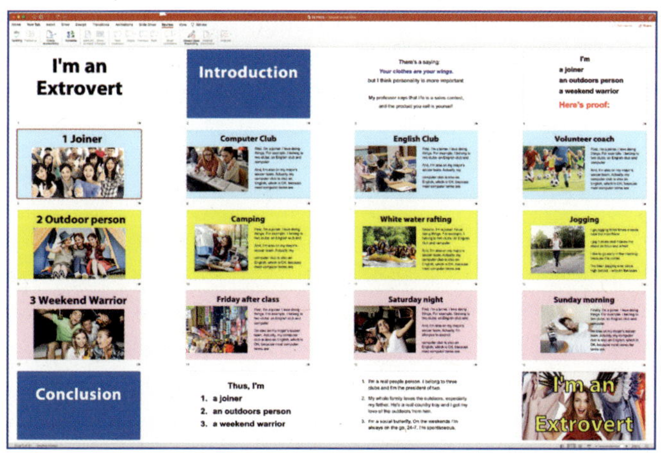

★ SAVE YOUR TEMPLATE ★

For your first presentation you create everything new. Colors, slides, font, size, color, alignment, margins, transitions. That takes time. After you finish, SAVE your presentation as a template. This will save all your formatting.

For your next presentation, open the template, give it a new name, and insert your new text and photos. Bada-bing! You finish is 1/3 the time. But no matter how long it takes you to make the presentation, you must practice at least 10 times.

Who's voice did they choose to save the planet?

Jennifer Lawrence

Wait a minute. That's a beautiful woman. Why would they chose a beauty, when they need a great voice?

SHE HAS A GREAT VOICE. That's why. Her persuasive voice is the reason she was chosen. There's a lot of beautiful women in Hollywood. Her voice is why she's a rich, famous and great actress.

How's your voice?

In 2016 the documentary ***A Beautiful Planet*** was released. It with filmed with super high-tech IMAX technology, with the cooperation of NASA. The documentary shows the effects of global warming. The movie hopes to help save the planet!

They have ONE chance to save the earth!

Of all the people on earth, who's voice did they select to narrate the movie?

Jennifer Lawrence.

Below are more stars who do voice work in the movies.
Beyoncé is also a singer, and Chris Rock and Eddie Murphy are also comedians. Their great voice helps them sell their songs and jokes. Their voices helped make them great.

Beyoncé

Mila Kunis

Cameron Diaz

Awkwafina

Michelle Yeoh

Sandra Bullock

Tom Hanks

Johnny Depp

Chris Rock

Hugh Jackman

Eddie Murphy

Chris Evans

How important is your voice to your career?

The highest paid sportscasters are not the best former players. They are the best speakers among the former players.

1 David Beckham is one of the most famous soccer players in the world.

Why isn't he a famous sportscaster? Why doesn't he cover the World Cup and the Olympics? Some people say it's because of his squeaky voice. His career is limited by his voice. To be clear, he's good-looking, popular and talented. He's a great guy, great father, great husband. His wife used to be a Spice Girl!

However, his career is limited by his voice, his speaking ability.

2 Malala Yousafzai won the Nobel Peace Price when she was 17.

She was born in a small town in Pakistan. When she was 15 years old, she was shot in the head by the Taliban, but survived. When she was interviewed in the hospital by world new organizations, she spoke English. If she had not spoken English, it is doubtful her career would have led to the Nobel Prize.

Her English speaking ability greatly increased her opportunities in life.

3 Caroline Kennedy (no photo) is the daughter of a US President and a Harvard graduate.

At one point in her career, she thought about becoming a US Senator, and was interviewed by the press. In one 30-minute interview, she said "you know" 168 times. And so, some people made fun of her. Shortly after, she withdrew her attempt for the senate. Honestly, she was probably just nervous at the interview. However, her speaking ability at that conference limited her career.

If she had taken this course, and watched her video presentations, she would probably be US President by now.

Your voice is an indicator of your personality, intelligence, education and social class.

Are you a smart, confident, articulate speaker? Or a meek, insecure mumbler?

Years ago, a world expert American professor gave a lecture to a international audience.
His British graduate student assistant then added a few details. The professor then asked if there were any questions. There were questions, but strangely, all questions were addressed to the grad student! Why? The grad student had an articulate, upper-class, polished British accent. Some people thought he was the expert. They thought that higher speaking ability meant higher intelligence.

Do you ever watch CNN? Many of their newscasters have British accents. ***Why?*** Americans think that upper-class British accents sound intelligent and authoritative. British newscasters are not smarter, they sound smarter. CNN uses that.

Your voice, your speaking ability, is an indicator of your intelligence and your education.
How is it an indicator of your education? Well, for example, people from Scotland, Ireland and Australia often have a strong accent. If their education stops at high school, they retain that accent. However, if they graduate from university (especially with a MA or PhD) they usually lose much of their accent. The longer you are in the educational system, the more accent you lose. You rarely hear a person with a PhD speak with a strong accent. (Well, maybe Australia.)

In England there are many regional dialects. And since certain parts of England are prosperous, and others are not, dialect can be a socioeconomic indicator. Some accents imply that you are high income and highly educated, and other accents indicate you are low income and low educated.

What does your voice say about you?

VOICE IMPROVEMENT

Your voice is a big part of your personality and character.

Are you a smart, confident, articulate speaker? Or a meek, insecure mumbler?

How to improve your voice

1 **Don't say 'Uh'.** (This may take a lot of practice.)

2 **Speak LOWER and SLOWER.**

SLOWER Insecure people sometimes speak quickly, because they are worried that someone might interrupt or cut them off before they are finished. In broad strokes, insecure people tend to speak fast, confident secure people speak slower.

LOWER People who are nervous, scared, and panicked often speak high and fast. There are examples of this in the military. Therefore, military officers are trained to "**Speak low and slow.**" A high voice is a sign of panic, a low and slow voice is a voice of calm and confidence. If an officer is scared, his voice will scare his men. If an officer is calm, his voice will calm his soldiers.

3 **Speak from the NECK, not the NOSE**

A common problem for many people is they speak from high from their nose, rather than lower from their chest, or diaphragm. Speaking through the nose can also sound nasal.

A common solution for many people is to lower their voice by speaking through the diaphragm (chest) or even the neck. You could say, lower where your voice is produced. Anywhere lower than the nose.

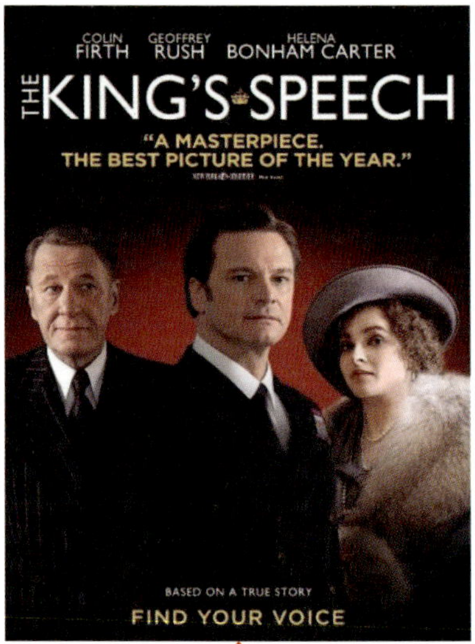

4 **Pronounce each syllable, and the ending of each word, distinctly. Crisp. Clear.**

Articulate. Enunciate. Pronounce each word, from beginning to end. **Do not mumble.** Take pride in each word, and pronounce it from beginning to end, clearly and distinctly. At the beginning, when you do this it will artificially slow. As you get better, you can speed it up (like with anything else).

If you think improving your voice is difficult, watch *The King's Speech.*

How do K-Pop groups improve their singing and dancing?

They practice a lot! 10 hours a day, 6 days a week. That's 60 hours a week.

At a glance, you can tell that top K-Pop groups have practiced many, many hours.

In your whole life, how many minutes, how many hours, have you actually SPOKEN English?

Do you ever watch English-language reality TV shows?

There are shows about travel, car repair, home building, real estate, pawn shops, cooking, travel, and being in the wilderness. There's even a show of people catching snakes! Frankly, many of them are not good looking. But, do you know what they all have in common? **They speak clearly.**

It's not rocket science. Skills are improved by hours and hours of repetitive practice. Watch any K-pop group.

You're in a race against time!

The older you get, the harder it is improve pronunciation.

That's **Arnold Swarzenneger and Jackie Chan**. They both started practicing English pronunciation when they were 20.

Arnold's from Austria, and moved to the US when he was 20. He's been making English movies for over 50 years. That's 50 years of speaking English, and rehearsing movie lines.
How's his pronunciation?

Jackie's been making English movies for almost 30 years. That's way older than you! You can be sure that he practiced his English movie lines many, many times.
How his pronunciation?

What's the point?

The point is: **PRACTICE NOW**. The older you get, the harder it is, and the longer it takes.

Practicing for 50 years

Practicing for 30 years

You spend 2 hours a day texting. Spend 20 minutes a day practicing pronunciation.

How to improve pronunciation?

The exact same way you improve anything. **Repetition**. The more you repeat, the better you get.

Let's say your major is **Architecture**, which is a little tricky to pronounce. You have 2 choices:

1. You can go through the rest of your life pronouncing is poorly.
2. You can go to **dictionary.com**, and click on the sound icon. 🔊 This will pronounce the word.

Architecture R-key-tec-sure 🔊

Listen and repeat, 100 times. ***100 times?*** It's your major, you should pronounce it correctly! So, your choice. Practice 100 times (it takes 5 minutes) and do it right for the rest of your life. Or do it wrong for the rest of your life.

Here's some sounds that Asian students have trouble with. They were on your placement test. You can go to the website and practice on the Pronunciation Page.

L	R	N	W
lack	rack	nack	wack
late	rate	Nate	wait
lay	ray	nay	way
lead	read	need	weed
leak	reek	neek	week

B	P	F	V
bail	pale	fail	veil
ban	pan	fan	van
bar	par	far	var
bare	pair	fare	vare
base	pace	face	vase

i	æ	ɛ	ɪ
bead	bad	bed	bid
beat	bat	bet	bit
cheap	chap	chep	chip
deed	dad	dead	did
eat	at	et	it

G, J	Ch	Z	Sh
gin	chin	zen	shin
Jane	chain	Zane	Shane
gyp	chip	zip	ship
jew	chew	zoo	shoe
Joe	Cho	Zoh	show

Pick the top 10 words in your major and pronounce them 100 times.
You can sound fluent, before you are fluent.

CONVERSATION SEMINAR

Dogs chase balls.
People like to talk about themselves.

It's Easy As 1, 2, 3

1 The Book. *Write what you will say.*

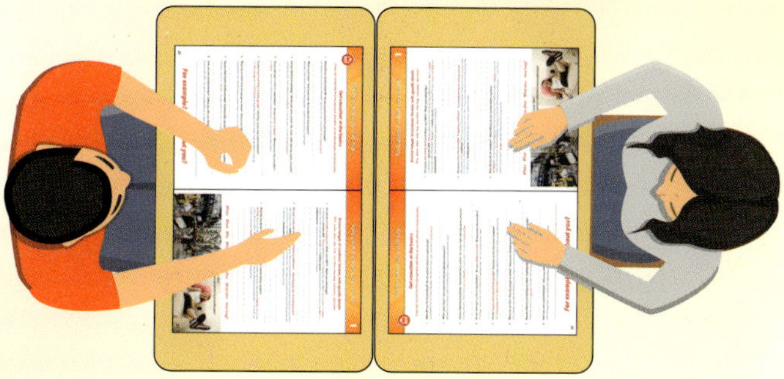

2 The Class. *Talk about what you wrote.*

3 The Test. *Transcribe and self-correct.*

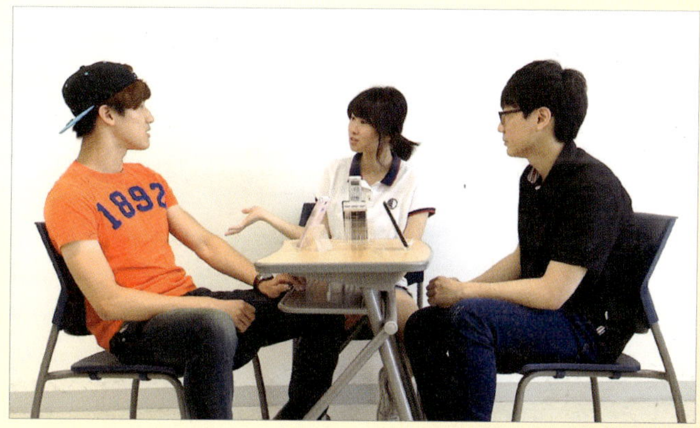

The Result

	Average words per utterance	Total words I spoke
Midterm test	10	400
Final test	17.5	500
Improvement	**75%**	**25%**

You improve, and you can prove it

1ST DAY PLACEMENT TEST

How can you improve your ability if you don't know your ability?

The test takes 15 minutes to give and grade, and it's more accurate than the 3-hour SAT test.

INSTRUCTIONS

1. Teachers push PLAY.
2. Students mark their answers on the answer sheet.
3. Students then enter their answers on their phone.
4. Google grades it in 2 minutes. Wow.

Teacher opens Excel and pushes SORT. ***Bada-bing***. In the first 20 minutes on the first day of class, teachers know the ability of student, which gives your your first conversation test partners.

9:05 am, the test starts

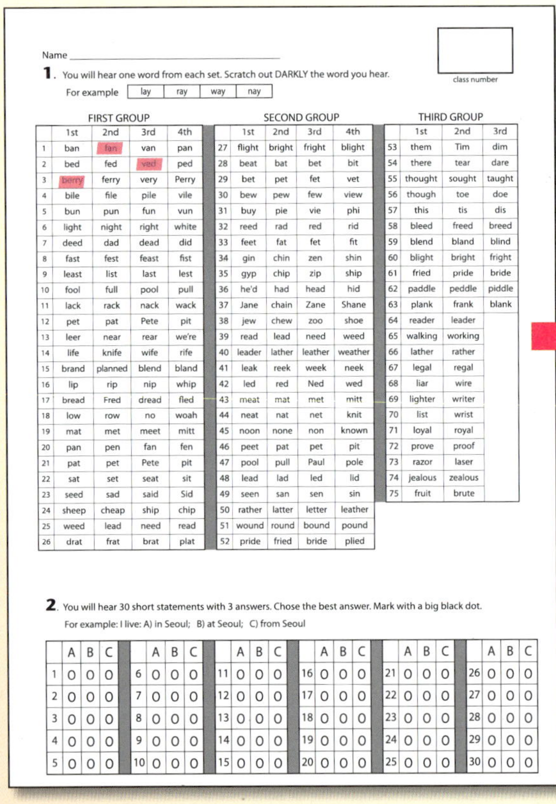

Name ______________________ (class number)

1. You will hear one word from each set. Scratch out DARKLY the word you hear.

For example | lay | ray | way | nay |

FIRST GROUP

	1st	2nd	3rd	4th
1	ban	fan	van	pan
2	bed	fed	ved	ped
3	berry	ferry	very	Perry
4	bile	file	pile	vile
5	bun	pun	fun	vun
6	light	night	right	white
7	deed	dad	dead	did
8	fast	fest	feast	fist
9	least	list	last	lest
10	fool	full	pool	pull
11	lack	rack	nack	wack
12	pet	pat	Pete	pit
13	leer	near	rear	we're
14	life	knife	wife	rife
15	brand	planned	blend	bland
16	lip	rip	nip	whip
17	bread	Fred	dread	fled
18	low	row	no	woah
19	mat	met	meet	mitt
20	pan	pen	fan	fen
21	pat	pet	Pete	pit
22	sat	set	seat	sit
23	seed	sad	said	Sid
24	sheep	cheap	ship	chip
25	weed	lead	need	read
26	drat	frat	brat	plat

SECOND GROUP

	1st	2nd	3rd	4th
27	flight	bright	fright	blight
28	beat	bat	bet	bit
29	bet	pet	fet	vet
30	bew	pew	few	view
31	buy	pie	vie	phi
32	reed	rad	red	rid
33	feet	fat	fet	fit
34	gin	chin	zen	shin
35	gyp	chip	zip	ship
36	he'd	had	head	hid
37	Jane	chain	Zane	Shane
38	jew	chew	zoo	shoe
39	read	lead	need	weed
40	leader	lather	leather	weather
41	leak	reek	week	neek
42	led	red	Ned	wed
43	meat	mat	met	mitt
44	neat	nat	net	knit
45	noon	none	non	known
46	peet	pat	pet	pit
47	pool	pull	Paul	pole
48	lead	lad	led	lid
49	seen	san	sen	sin
50	rather	latter	letter	leather
51	wound	round	bound	pound
52	pride	fried	bride	plied

THIRD GROUP

	1st	2nd	3rd
53	them	Tim	dim
54	there	tear	dare
55	thought	sought	taught
56	though	toe	doe
57	this	tis	dis
58	bleed	freed	breed
59	blend	bland	blind
60	blight	bright	fright
61	fried	pride	bride
62	paddle	peddle	piddle
63	plank	frank	blank
64	reader	leader	
65	walking	working	
66	lather	rather	
67	legal	regal	
68	liar	wire	
69	lighter	writer	
70	list	wrist	
71	loyal	royal	
72	prove	proof	
73	razor	laser	
74	jealous	zealous	
75	fruit	brute	

2. You will hear 30 short statements with 3 answers. Chose the best answer. Mark with a big black dot.

For example: I live: A) in Seoul; B) at Seoul; C) from Seoul

	A	B	C		A	B	C		A	B	C		A	B	C		A	B	C		A	B	C
1	O	O	O	6	O	O	O	11	O	O	O	16	O	O	O	21	O	O	O	26	O	O	O
2	O	O	O	7	O	O	O	12	O	O	O	17	O	O	O	22	O	O	O	27	O	O	O
3	O	O	O	8	O	O	O	13	O	O	O	18	O	O	O	23	O	O	O	28	O	O	O
4	O	O	O	9	O	O	O	14	O	O	O	19	O	O	O	24	O	O	O	29	O	O	O
5	O	O	O	10	O	O	O	15	O	O	O	20	O	O	O	25	O	O	O	30	O	O	O

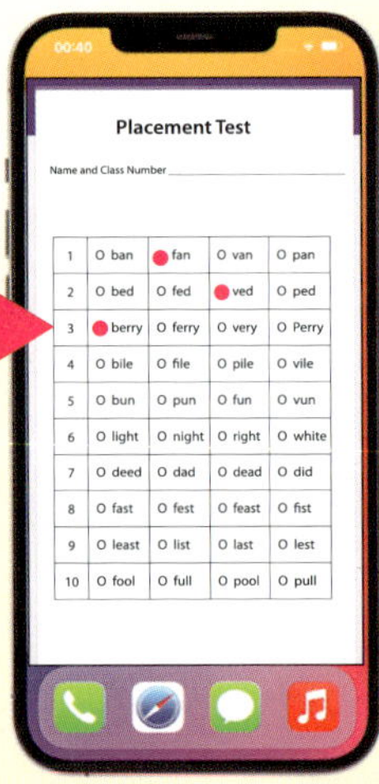

9:20 am, Score & 1st Test Partners

Score			
99 92 90	10 Kwon, Ho hyuk	9 Koo, Hee bo	13 Lee, Hyun min
89 88 87	4 Hong, So he	5 Jeong, Soo min	7 Kim, Kyun hee
85 83 80	8 Kim, Won su	3 Choi, Lee so	19 PARK, Min hee
79 78 76	2 Choi, Pak lee	14 Lee, Jang soo	15 Lee, Kwon min
73 72 68	6 Kim, He suk	16 Park, Soo an	11 Kwon, Min so
67 64 58	12 Jung, Ah jang	21 Park, Sung mo	18 PARK, Koo min
57 57 54	17 Park, Jang won	1 Ahn, Kun lee	20 PARK, Sin min

On the first day of class, teachers know your:

1. Speaking ability
2. Pronunciation problems
3. Prepositions problems
4. First conversation test partners →

That's a pretty good use of 20 minutes.

First test partners

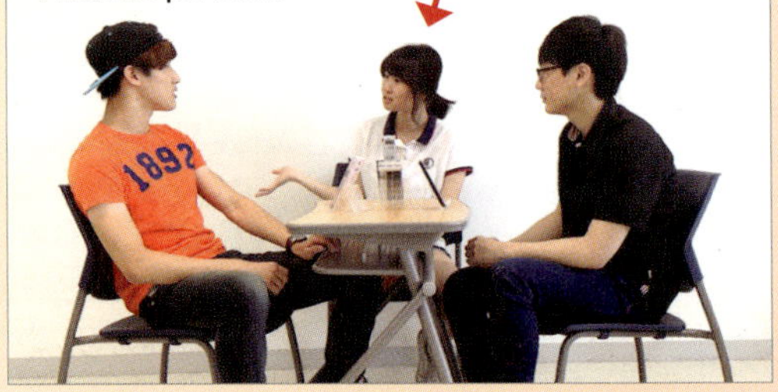

You've been taking English for 10 years. In 20 minutes, you'll know your ability.

The Engine of Improvement is Repetition

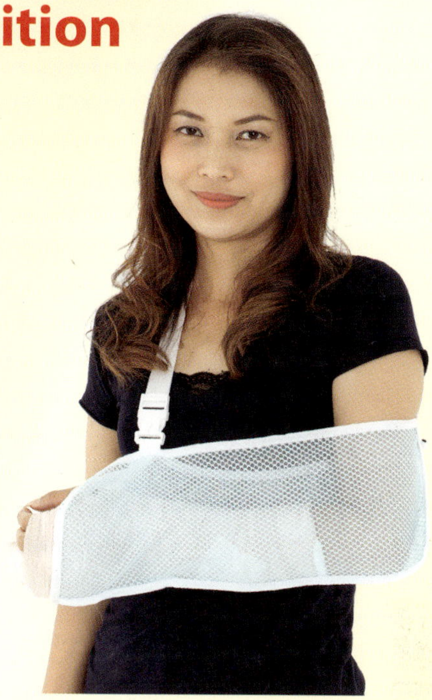

It works like this:

One day she came into class with a broken arm.
Her first partner asked, *What happened?*
Then her second partner, *What happened?*
Then her third. Every partner asked, *What happened?*
By the end of class, she was pretty good at explaining how she broke her arm.

In class conversations, you're not role playing about ordering a steak.
You get better at answering personally-relevant questions. Telling 10 or 20 partners why you chose your major is pretty good preparation for your conversation test.
And for life.

If you want to make a conversation 'academic' ask an academic question. ***Simple*****.**

In a class of 24, here's how to have 23 new partners in 4 classes.

Half your partners are better speakers, and they all bring new knowledge, vocabulary and pronunciation

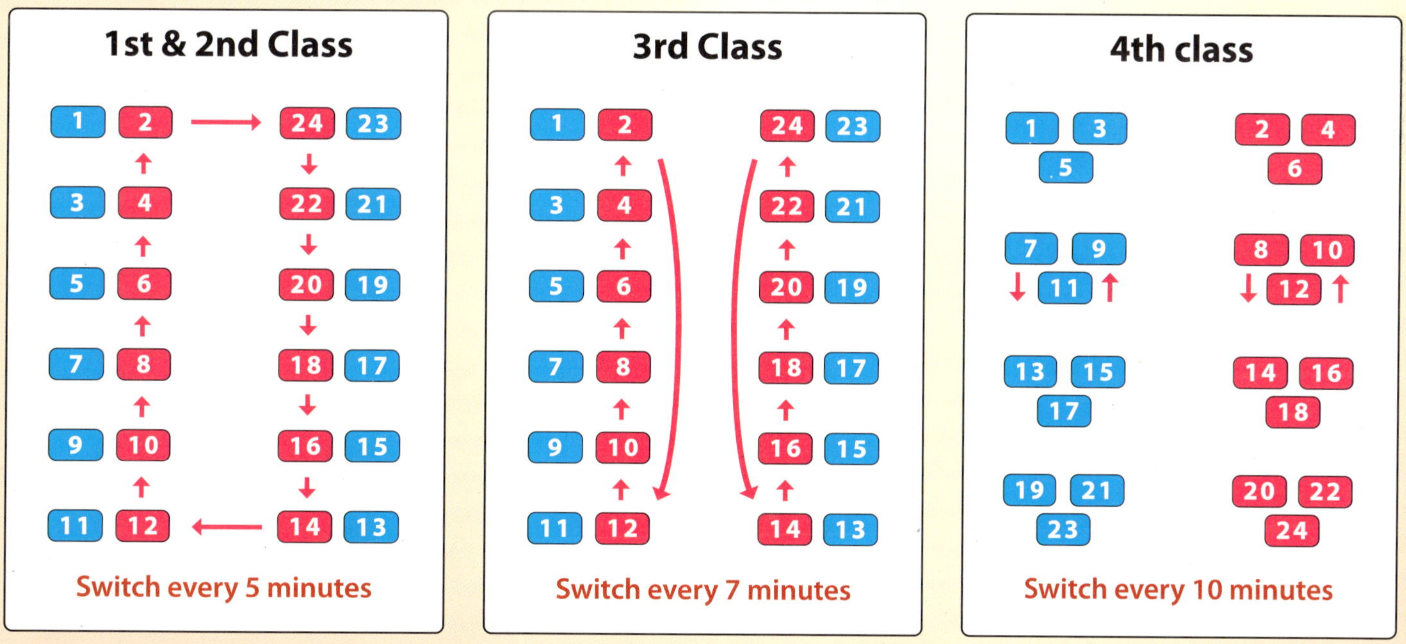

Wow, that's about 4 hours of English conversations.

Yes, and if you're a freshman maybe the whole class is total strangers. That's a lot of possible new best friends.
What will you talk about? Your **major**, your **schedule**, your **club**, your **presentation**, what you did **last weekend**.

This is not goofing off. This is systematic improvement.
Many partners make you smoother, better partners make you better.

1st Conversation Test

The first test gives your Ability and your second test partners.

MS Word can measure speaking ability. It's as easy as 1, 2, 3.

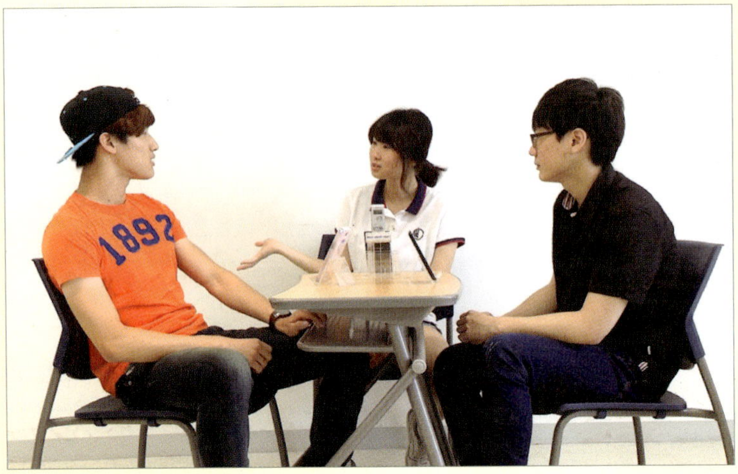

1

1. Three students of similar ability have a 17-minute conversation.
2. Record it with your phone.
3. Students transcribe just what you said on MS Word (about 2 hours).
4. MS Word gives how many words you spoke, and how many times you spoke.
5. Simple division gives your average words-per-turn.

2

Type just what you said. It takes 2 hours or less. Email or upload.

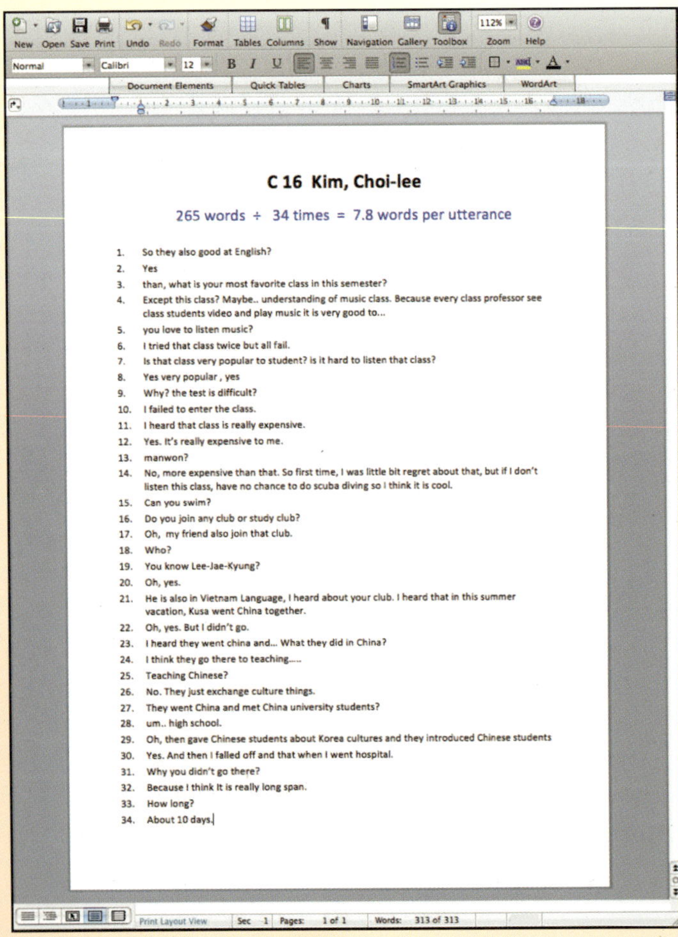

C 16 Kim, Choi-lee

265 words ÷ 34 times = 7.8 words per utterance

1. So they also good at English?
2. Yes
3. than, what is your most favorite class in this semester?
4. Except this class? Maybe.. understanding of music class. Because every class professor see class students video and play music it is very good to...
5. you love to listen music?
6. I tried that class twice but all fail.
7. Is that class very popular to student? is it hard to listen that class?
8. Yes very popular , yes
9. Why? the test is difficult?
10. I failed to enter the class.
11. I heard that class is really expensive.
12. Yes. It's really expensive to me.
13. manwon?
14. No, more expensive than that. So first time, I was little bit regret about that, but if I don't listen this class, have no chance to do scuba diving so I think it is cool.
15. Can you swim?
16. Do you join any club or study club?
17. Oh, my friend also join that club.
18. Who?
19. You know Lee-Jae-Kyung?
20. Oh, yes.
21. He is also in Vietnam Language, I heard about your club. I heard that in this summer vacation, Kusa went China together.
22. Oh, yes. But I didn't go.
23. I heard they went china and... What they did in China?
24. I think they go there to teaching.....
25. Teaching Chinese?
26. No. They just exchange culture things.
27. They went China and met China university students?
28. um.. high school.
29. Oh, then gave Chinese students about Korea cultures and they introduced Chinese students
30. Yes. And then I failed off and that when I went hospital.
31. Why you didn't go there?
32. Because I think It is really long span.
33. How long?
34. About 10 days.

3

Total words spoken on the first test gives your **second test partners**.

Total Words	2nd Test Partners		
695, 668, 643	6 Kim, He suk	1 Ahn, Kun lee	18 PARK, Koo min
582, 564, 544	4 Hong, So he	5 Jeong, Soo min	7 Kim, Kyun hee
521, 509, 453	8 Kim, Won su	3 Choi, Lee so	19 PARK, Min hee
421, 421, 398	2 Choi, Pak lee	14 Lee, Jang soo	15 Lee, Kwon min
367, 345, 321	17 Park, Jang won	16 Park, Soo an	11 Kwon, Min so
288, 267, 245	12 Jung, Ah jang	21 Park, Sung mo	20 PARK, Sin min
180, 167, 149	10 Kwon, Ho hyuk	9 Koo, Hee bo	13 Lee, Hyun min

Partners of similar ability make the second test fair, and even more accurate.

2ND CONVERSATION TEST

The second test gives your Ability and Improvement.

B20 Kim, Me-lee

	How many times I spoke	Average words per turn	Total words I spoke
Midterm test	**46**	**8.6**	**400**
Final test	**54**	**15.5**	**480**
	Improvement	**80%**	**20%**

Thus, my speaking improved 50% this semester.

VOCABULARY

ROMANCE	PART-TIME JOB	FREE TIME
love at first sight	workaholic	weekend warrior
high maintenance	cash poor	couch potato
ghost	flunky	spontaneous
pretty boy	materialistic	social butterfly
henpecked		

The top 5 mistakes and how to fix them.

1. No, I didn't heard about that.
   No, I didn't hear about that.
2. I have never been gone to there.
   I've never been there.
3. I am interesting in that.
   I am interested in that major.
4. What is your best favorite movie?
   What is your favorite movie?
5. Will you go to a festival or them park on this winter vacation?
   Will you go to any festivals or theme park this winter vacation?

---

1. Usually I'm weekend warriors, but last weekend I stayed at home because this week is midterm exam, so I was staying at home and studying for midterm exam. What did you do last weekend?
2. No, I didn't heard about that.
3. Last weekend I was couch potato. What about you?
4. I don't like gory films. I like superhero movies, like the Avengers and Ironman.

When you compare your first and second test data, you'll see your speaking improvement.

INSTRUCTIONS

1. **Show up** on time, and have a conversation with your new partners.
2. **Download** the example MS Word transcript, and insert your own information.
3. **Underline** the idioms you used, and copy and paste them onto the first page.
4. **Highlight** your top 5 mistakes, and copy and past them onto the first page.
5. **Enter** your data.

What about mistakes?

When you transcribe, you HEAR, TYPE and READ every mistake you made.

AND!

Transcribing the second test usually takes less time. You speak more, but you're better at transcribing.

This is a communicative test. And **MS Word** measures precisely how much, and how much more, you communicated.

Before & After Checklist

Use this checklist to make sure your presentation is done correctly.
You can also use it to start Feedback Conversations.
For unit 1, put checks in column 1. Add so on.

VOICE	1	2	3	4	5	6
1. *Do I speak in a clear confident voice?*						
2. *Do I speak to fast or too slow?*						
3. *Is my pronunciation crisp and clear?*						
4. *Is my voice too high? Too nasal?*						
5. *Do I add emphasis and excitement with my voice?*						
6. *How is the audio quality?*						
7. *How many times do I say "Uh"?*						
INTRO AND ENDING						
8. *Is the introduction interesting?*						
9. *Is there an interesting hook?*						
10. *Does the conclusion mirror the introduction?*						
11. *Does it have a boffo ending?*						
12. *Is the conclusion dramatic, or it just faded away?*						
13. *Are the specific examples clear? Interesting?*						
14. *Is there something that should have been added?*						
15. *Is there something that should have been left out?*						
SLIDES						
16. *Are the headlines too big? Big enough?*						
17. *Is the background color to dark or too busy?*						
18. *Is there too much text on the slides?*						
19. *Is the text too small? Too ornate? Too boring?*						
20. *Are the slide transitions smooth and consistent?*						
21. *Are the section transitions dramatic? Too fast or slow?*						
22. *Are there too many different kinds of transitions?*						
23. *Are the slide color, type, border, etc, consistent?*						
OVERALL						
24. *Does the presentation persuade you? Bore you?*						
25. *Do I take pride in my work?*						
26. *Does it look like I practiced at least 10 times?*						
27. *Do I sound like a professional announcer?*						
28. *Would you pay to watch it again?*						
29. *Did I send it to 1 or 2 friends or family to watch?*						
30. *Did I watch it myself on YouTube to make sure it uploaded OK?*						

Notes & Scratch Pad

She has a passion for fashion.

And it shows.

Idiom Quiz

Improve your LISTENING and VOCABULARY at the same time.

1. You will hear a short sentence with 3 possible answers, **A**, **B**, **C**. Mark the best answer with a big, black dot.
2. For example: A party pooper . . . **A**) Likes to party. **B**) Leaves a party early. **C**) Is tired all the time.
3. Mark your answers on this page then go to the website and enter them there.

To really increase your improvement, you could . . .

1. Listen and repeat, then listen and answer.
2. Listen, repeat and record yourself, then listen to yourself and answer.
3. Listen and transcribe on MS Word, then answer. MS Word will correct your spelling. And, **listening to**, **reading**, and **typing** the idiom will help you master it.

	1 Personality			2 Education			3 Technology			4 Romance			5 Part-time Job			6 Free Time		
	A	B	C	A	B	C	A	B	C	A	B	C	A	B	C	A	B	C
1	○	○	○	○	○	○	○	○	○	○	○	○	○	○	○	○	○	○
2	○	○	○	○	○	○	○	○	○	○	○	○	○	○	○	○	○	○
3	○	○	○	○	○	○	○	○	○	○	○	○	○	○	○	○	○	○
4	○	○	○	○	○	○	○	○	○	○	○	○	○	○	○	○	○	○
5	○	○	○	○	○	○	○	○	○	○	○	○	○	○	○	○	○	○
6	○	○	○	○	○	○	○	○	○	○	○	○	○	○	○	○	○	○
7	○	○	○	○	○	○	○	○	○	○	○	○	○	○	○	○	○	○
8	○	○	○	○	○	○	○	○	○	○	○	○	○	○	○	○	○	○
9	○	○	○	○	○	○	○	○	○	○	○	○	○	○	○	○	○	○
10	○	○	○	○	○	○	○	○	○	○	○	○	○	○	○	○	○	○
Score																		

Listen, repeat, transcribe, and then answer. Transcribing on a computer will improve your English typing skills.

Notes & Scratch Pad

You can do it!

Idiom Index

If you want more information about an idiom, or how to pronounce it, you can go to: dictionary.com

IDIOM INDEX

After every unit, highlight the vocabulary you learned.
After every conversation test, highlight the vocabulary you used.

Conversation Based
LEARNING
• PUBLISHING COMPANY •
Because life is not a grammar test

Jangchungdan-ro 8-gil 59-22, Jung-gu, Seoul, Korea 04614
PlanGBro@gmail.com • ConversationBasedLearning.com

Published and printed in South Korea, 2023

ISBN: 979-11-88562-15-2

Editors: Stephanie Ptak and Andrea Lee
Design & Layout: Gunther Breaux
Photo credits: ©Bigstock,

ACKNOWLEDGEMENTS

Amy Aleha's audio recording contribution is greatly appreciated. She makes this book possible.

I would like to thank: Stephanie Ptak, Andrea Lee, Sean Dailey, Max Watson, Shaun Manning, Jim Life, Rhea Metituk, Stephen Walker, Daniel Rhodes and Daniel Deacon, who gave me the great benefits of their experience and expertise.

Gui Lim Kang's help in design and teaching methodology has enhanced this work.

Gunther Breaux has taught English Conversation to university students in Korea for 25 years. He's presented at international conferences in Korea, Japan, China, Hong Kong, Thailand, England and the United States. He has taught Business English at the Korea Development Institute (KDI) Graduate School of Public Policy and Management, and Computer Graphics at the Korea National University of the Arts. His original thought and contribution to English Education is Conversation Based Learning.

He has a BA in Advertising Design, an MA in American History, and an MATESOL. Before Korea, Gunther's job history included commercial artist, art director at an advertising agency, bartender, dancing instructor, diver, welder and tugboat captain. He has run five full marathons and has a black belt in Taekwondo. He's an interesting guy who knows the value of interesting teaching materials. He also knows that life is a contest of passion and ability. His books give you the ability to express your passion in English.

Contact the author: **PlanGBro@gmail.com**

For more books by Gunther Breaux go to: **ConversationBasedLearning.com**

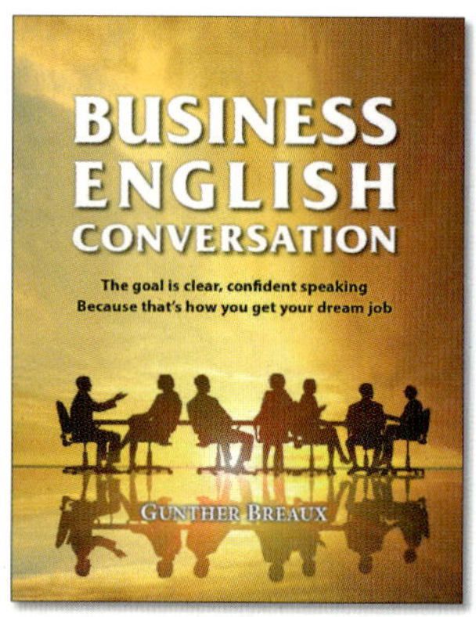